Early Praise for *Test-Driven React: Second Edition*

Test-Driven React goes into great detail on how to set up testing React components in modern applications. By following the steps Trevor has clearly outlined, you'll be up and testing in no time.

➤ **Kent C. Dodds**
Creator of React Testing Library

This book offers more than just theory. It provides a concrete, practical guide to seamlessly integrating TDD into your React development process.

➤ **David Mansy**
Front-end Engineer, Amazon

Test-Driven React is a masterclass in setting up a productive development workflow, in such a simple, clear, and concise language that it's a joy to read and reread.

➤ **Tibor Simic**
Senior Developer, IBM

This book goes far beyond just teaching tools and approaches to test React—which it does very thoroughly. It also shows common production code pitfalls and their solutions. It is a great resource for anyone from "I just worked through my first React tutorial" to "I am a seasoned pro but might not be up-to-date on the state of the art."

➤ **Henrik Horneber**
Senior Software Engineer, Continental Reifen Deutschland GmbH

Praise for the First Edition

Test-Driven React is a great hands-on introduction to the latest technologies in front-end development. Even if you have little experience with React and front-end testing, the detailed examples in this book will guide you every step of the way to creating working and tested code.

➤ **Ludovico Fischer**
   Author of *React for Real*

Twenty-first century web app development (especially in React) can easily become a morass of npm dependencies, copy-pasted Stack Overflow code, and general kludginess. Fortunately, there is hope in the shape of test-driven development (TDD): write a failing test, make it pass, refactor, repeat. Trevor Burnham's *Test-Driven React* will help lead you back from the brink so you can make web development pleasurable again.

➤ **Richard Murnane**
   Software Developer, 3P Learning

This is an incredibly comprehensive guide to improving the testing and development workflows of React developers at any experience level. Whether you're looking to test a React component for the first time or rework your testing workflow after years in the industry, *Test Driven React*'s engaging and interactive lessons will fundamentally change how you think about JavaScript testing.

➤ **Adam Markon**
   Software Engineer, HubSpot

Test-Driven React, Second Edition

Find Problems Early, Fix Them Quickly,
Code with Confidence

Trevor Burnham

The Pragmatic Bookshelf

Dallas, Texas

For our complete catalog of hands-on, practical, and Pragmatic content for software developers, please visit *https://pragprog.com*.

Contact *support@pragprog.com* for sales, volume licensing, and support.

For international rights, please contact *rights@pragprog.com*.

The team that produced this book includes:

Publisher:	Dave Thomas
COO:	Janet Furlow
Executive Editor:	Susannah Davidson
Development Editor:	Jacquelyn Carter
Copy Editor:	L. Sakhi MacMillan
Indexing:	Potomac Indexing, LLC
Layout:	Gilson Graphics

ISBN-13: 979-8-88865-065-3
Book version: P1.0—September 2024

Contents

Acknowledgments

This book wouldn't have been possible without the help of many people. The lion's share of the thanks belongs to my editor at the Pragmatic Bookshelf, Jackie Carter, for pushing this project forward. Thanks to everyone who took the time to provide a technical review: Oleh Boreiko, Ludovico Fischer, Henrik Horneber, David Mansy, Anton Matyulkov, Chris Mendis, and Tibor Simic. Thanks as well to everyone who reported errata during the beta.

For the fifth time, I've had the privilege of writing under the Pragmatic Bookshelf banner. I owe a debt of gratitude to the Pragmatic team for taking a chance on me back when I was starting out. Every book we've managed to produce together is a minor miracle.

This book is dedicated to the open source community. Without their work, the amazing tools and libraries that make modern web development such a joy simply wouldn't exist. To learn how you can support the developers whose free code powers your projects, use the `npm fund` command.

Introduction

I vividly remember the first time I wrote code. I was ten years old and utterly obsessed with robots. The local public library must have lent me every book they had on the subject. One of those books had an appendix, "Write Your Own Robot in BASIC." I ran to my parents' computer, fired up qbasic (bundled with the cutting-edge MS-DOS operating system), and fed in the instructions for my robot companion.

The program was unimpressive by today's standards. It was a primitive version of what we would now call a "chatbot." It would give you a prompt like this one:

```
>>> Greetings, human. How are you feeling today?
```

Then it would wait for you to enter a recognizable string like tired and give an appropriate response, something like this:

```
>>> I am sorry to hear that. How about a nice cup of coffee?
```

And it would continue. The only keywords in the entire program were IF, THEN, and GOTO.

Even though my chatbot wouldn't stand a snowball's chance in a Turing test, the exercise was a revelation to me: I could actually *create* something just by *typing.* Now it seemed that robots were old news. Computers were where it's at!

As computers have grown more capable, software has grown more complex, and that thrilling feeling has become more elusive. New layers of abstraction have empowered me to do more with less code but at the cost of constant uncertainty: *will my code do what I intended?*

Test-driven development (TDD) is the art of minimizing that uncertainty, allowing you to feel confident about your code from the moment you write it. How? By making a few assertions about that code beforehand. This groundwork sets up a short, satisfying feedback loop: as soon as you write your code, the tests light up green. Afterward the tests remain in place, standing guard against regressions.

I don't always use TDD, but when I do, I feel a little bit closer to the magic of that first coding experience. All of the rigamarole of modern software development fades away. I can focus all my energies on reaching toward the green light.

What's in This Book

This is a book about React. But it's not like any other book about React. This is a book about writing React code in a joyful way. You might learn a few new things about React, but that's not my goal. My goal is to help you write better code and to have more fun doing it.

In Chapter 1, Test-Driven Development with Jest, on page 1, you'll get a taste of test-driven development, a programming methodology that uses tests to create a feedback loop as you work. You'll meet Jest, a lightning-fast test framework which is the perfect companion for TDD.

Chapter 2, Integrated Tooling with VS Code, on page 17, will introduce you to some of my favorite tools: VS Code, an amazingly powerful editor; Type-Script, a dramatic enhancement to the JavaScript language; and ESLint and Prettier, the ultimate code beautification duo. You'll experience the wonder of instantaneous feedback as you code.

Then in Chapter 3, Testing React with Testing Library, on page 45, you'll start writing React components and testing them with the aptly named React Testing Library. You'll build a complex component the TDD way.

Chapter 4, Styling in JavaScript with Styled-Components, on page 77, is all about style. You'll use the styled-components library to add pizzazz to your React components without the need for separate CSS files. You'll also learn about testing styles and using one of Jest's most powerful features: snapshots.

In Chapter 5, Refactoring with Hooks, on page 101, you'll learn some important techniques for refactoring React components. You'll extract pieces of functionality into hooks, encouraging code reuse and allowing core components to stay small and easy to test. And you'll look at your components with X-ray vision through the power of the React Devtools.

Finally, in Chapter 6, Continuous Integration and Collaboration, on page 123, you'll meet all the tools you'll need to share what you've built with the world. You'll run your tests in the cloud with Travis CI, enforce your project's rules with Husky, and create beautiful, interactive documentation with Storybook.

What's Not in This Book

This is not an introduction to JavaScript. If you're new to the language, or if you just want a refresher, I highly recommend Kyle Simpson's excellent *You Don't Know JS Yet*[1] series. Most of the code in this book will employ features added to the language as part of the ECMAScript 6 (also known as ES6 or ES2015) standard. Here's a quick test:

```
const stringifyAll = (...args) => args.map(String);
```

If any of that syntax is confounding, you'll find clarity in Simpson's series.

We'll also be using TypeScript. TypeScript is a superset of JavaScript that adds type annotations. The syntax may look strange at first, but the examples in this book should be fairly easy to understand. If you're interested in diving deeper, I recommend *Learning TypeScript [Gol22]* by Josh Goldberg.

Some familiarity with React is helpful, but not required. I'll give a brief explanation for each React concept we encounter. If you feel lost, a good resource is *React Quickly [BM23]* by Morten Barklund and Azat Mardan.

All tests in this book are unit tests, meaning the JavaScript code is tested in isolation. In production applications, I highly recommend adding functional tests using a tool like Playwright[2] in addition to unit tests.

Unit Tests vs. Functional Tests

Unit tests, by definition, test a single unit of code (such as a React component) in isolation. Nothing outside of that unit should affect whether the test passes or fails. But that's not how code works in the real world! In the context of a real application, whether your component works or not is likely to depend on the behavior of other components, on data returned by APIs, and on countless other factors.

So why write unit tests at all? Two reasons. First, unit tests are much faster. For TDD, it's critical to get feedback in seconds, not minutes. Second, unit tests are easier to write. That's why I recommend starting with unit tests, then adding functional tests after you have a working application (but before shipping it to production!).

Even as your application's functional requirements change, many of its components will remain the same, so unit tests will continue to provide value. Functional tests, on the other hand, will need to be rewritten as the application evolves.

---

1. https://github.com/getify/You-Dont-Know-JS
2. https://playwright.dev

What's New in the Second Edition

React development has seen an incredible evolution from 2019 to 2023, with dramatic improvements for both the developer experience and the results we can deliver to users. This edition reflects many of those improvements.

The most obvious change is the shift from JavaScript to TypeScript, Microsoft's typechecked JavaScript superset. TypeScript was a bleeding-edge technology back in 2019; today it's the industry standard for writing reliable code. Once you start using TypeScript, you'll wonder how you ever did without it! All of the React code in this book is now in TypeScript, and TypeScript concepts are explained for newcomers.

React code looks very different now than it did a few years ago, thanks to the addition of hooks in React 16.8. Hooks are a powerful feature that allows stateful components to be defined as a single function instead of a class. Additionally, hooks are a neat way of encapsulating reusable functionality across components. The chapter originally entitled "Refactoring with Higher-Order Components" has been replaced with one called Chapter 5, Refactoring with Hooks, on page 101, and all React code has been updated to reflect best practices as of React 18.

On the testing side of things, the Enzyme framework has fallen in popularity in favor of the simply named React Testing Library. It offers a conceptually different approach to testing React components: instead of making assertions about a component's state or the React tree it generates, you fully render the component and look at the resulting DOM tree. This approach to React testing has proven more intuitive (and less finicky) and is embraced in this edition.

Lastly, we've seen a revolution in web application build tools and frameworks in the last few years. The first edition of this book walked readers through the process of setting up a build chain with Webpack and Babel, step by step. Today there are a number of "batteries included" frameworks that require little to no configuration to compile modern React code. Some, like Next.js[3] and Remix,[4] are full-stack frameworks with a built-in Node.js instance for server-side rendering (SSR). This edition uses Vite,[5] a lightweight alternative to Webpack with a highly performant integrated testing library, Vitest.

---

3. https://nextjs.org/
4. https://remix.run/
5. https://vitejs.dev/

How to Read the Code Examples

This book takes a hands-on, project-driven approach, which means that source files often change over the course of a chapter. When a code example is a work in progress, its file name (relative to the project root) is shown as a comment at the top of the snippet:

```
// src/MyComponent.test.tsx
import { render, screen } from "@testing-library/react";
import MyComponent from "./MyComponent";

describe("MyComponent", () => {
  it("renders a <div>", () => {
    render(<MyComponent />);
    expect(screen.getByRole("div")).toBeInTheDocument();
  });
});
```

As a source file changes over the course of a chapter, familiar sections are omitted with ... and new/edited lines are highlighted:

```
// src/MyComponent.test.tsx
...
describe("MyComponent", () => {
  ...
  it("accepts a `className` prop", () => {
    render(<MyComponent className="test-class" />);
    expect(screen.getByRole("div")).toHaveClass("test-class");
  });
});
```

The final version of a source file within a chapter has a download link at the top instead of a comment:

```
intro/src/MyComponent.test.tsx
import { render, screen } from "@testing-library/react";
import userEvent from "@testing-library/user-event";
import MyComponent from "./MyComponent";

describe("MyComponent", () => {
  it("renders a <div>", () => {
    render(<MyComponent />);
    expect(screen.getByRole("div")).toBeInTheDocument();
  });

  it("accepts a `className` prop", () => {
    render(<MyComponent className="test-class" />);
    expect(screen.getByRole("div")).toHaveClass("test-class");
  });

  it("triggers `onClick` when clicked", async () => {
    const onClick = vi.fn();
```

```
    render(<MyComponent onClick={onClick} />);
    const nextButton = screen.getByRole("button");
    const user = userEvent.setup();
    await user.click(nextButton);
    expect(onClick).toHaveBeenCalled();
  });
});
```

Online Resources

You can find the source code for the projects in this book on the PragProg website.[6] You can also use the site to report errata. Help make this book better for other readers!

Mantra: Code with Joy

At its best, coding is an exercise in imagination and exploration, an exciting journey into the unknown. At its worst, it feels like stumbling in the dark. Which kind of experience you'll have is largely determined by feedback. The next time you're feeling frustrated, take a step back and ask yourself what kind of feedback would help you move forward. What question can you ask about your code that would bring clarity? Can you turn that question into a test?

I hope this book will help you bring more joy to your work by instilling a habit of seeking feedback early and often. Let's begin!

Trevor Burnham
trevorburnham@gmail.com
Cambridge, MA, August 2024

---

6.   https://pragprog.com/titles/tbreact2

CHAPTER 1

Test-Driven Development with Jest

Most tests are an afterthought. A programmer writes hundreds of lines of code to add a new feature to an application, followed by a perfunctory test or two. This "test-later" way of working has several drawbacks.

First, without tests, the programmer receives no feedback while writing the feature. If their approach turns out to be a dead end, they won't know it until they've finished the entire implementation.

Second, the tests the programmer writes after implementing the feature tend to be unthorough and unimaginative. Typically they confirm that the feature works along the "happy path"—that is, when used exactly as anticipated—rather than revealing potential bugs that might occur under edge case conditions.

Lastly, the programmer will be tempted to graft the new feature onto the app rather than rethinking the existing app structure, leading to codebase bloat. Fear of breaking other functionality prevents them from refactoring.

Fortunately, there's an alternative: *write the tests first!* That's the core tenet of the software development methodology known as test-driven development (TDD). In addition to encouraging thorough test coverage, TDD changes the coding experience by giving you rapid feedback; with your tests already in place, you can quickly find out what works and what doesn't. That gives you the freedom to experiment with different approaches. Experimentation leads to learning, which leads to better code. Plus, it's just more fun!

This book will introduce you to a TDD workflow suited to React development. That means taking full advantage of the extensive range of tools that have joined the JavaScript ecosystem in the last few years: Jest, TypeScript, ESLint, Prettier, and more. Used properly, these tools will give you the feedback you need to rapidly write code that's both readable and reliable.

In this chapter, you'll build a simple JavaScript project using a test-driven approach. With Jest as your test framework, you'll be able to create a lightning-fast feedback loop. Along the way, you'll learn how to manage dependencies with npm.

Although this chapter's project is extremely simple, the tools introduced here will continue to serve you through the rest of the book. In Chapter 2, Integrated Tooling with VS Code, on page 17, you'll integrate these and other tools into the VS Code editor. All of this preparation will give you a strong foundation when you dive into React development in Chapter 3, Testing React with Testing Library, on page 45.

Let's start by setting up Node and npm on your computer and writing some tests using Jest.

Introducing Jest

Jest is a test framework developed by Meta (née Facebook). Thanks to its rich feature set and solid performance, it's become the most popular library for testing JavaScript code in recent years.

Jest vs. Vitest

This chapter introduces you to testing with Jest, due to its popularity and ease of setup. However, later chapters will use Vitest, a Jest alternative that offers even faster performance when used in tandem with the Vite build tool.

Vitest is designed for compatibility with tests written for Jest, so rest assured that the knowledge you pick up in this chapter will carry over!

Unlike its forerunners, which expect to run in a browser environment, Jest runs in a Node process. That may seem counterintuitive: shouldn't code written to be run in the browser be tested in the browser? Short answer—not anymore! It's become possible to simulate (most) browser APIs in Node, thanks to a miraculous library called jsdom.[1] The advantages of using a simulated browser environment in Node are huge: tests can be run much more quickly, code coverage can be calculated easily, and the same tests can be run on any system—whether it's a developer's laptop or a continuous integration server—with consistent results.

You'll be using Jest as your test framework throughout this book. In this section, you'll set up a Node project, add Jest as a dependency, and run your first test. No prior experience with Node is required, but you'll need some

---

1.   https://github.com/jsdom/jsdom

familiarity with the JavaScript language, including the ES6 arrow function syntax. If you need an introduction, or a refresher, check out Kyle Simpson's *You Don't Know JS.*[2]

Installing Node and npm

The JavaScript landscape has changed dramatically since the '00s, and nothing bears as much responsibility for all that change as Node.js ("Node" for short). JavaScript was created at Netscape in 1995 to run in one specific place—the browser. In the late '90s and early '00s, server-side JavaScript was attempted in various forms, but without much success. Then Node hit the scene in 2009. Its impact was dramatic. Today, JavaScript powers millions of servers, rivals Ruby and Python in popularity as a scripting language, and lies at the core of many rich desktop apps—including VS Code, a full-featured code editor you'll meet in the next chapter. Thanks to Node, JavaScript is *everywhere.*

Check if you have Node installed by running node -v:

```
$ node -v
v18.14.1
```

If that command runs and gives you version 18 or higher, you're good to go. If not, go to NodeJS.org[3] to download and install the latest LTS (long-term support) release. If it still doesn't run, you may need to add the node executable to your command-line shell's PATH.[4]

The Node installer should also have included an executable called npm:

```
$ npm -v
9.3.1
```

Officially, npm (never capitalized) is not an acronym. But colloquially, it's known as the node package manager. And as we'll soon see, it's an indispensable tool!

Creating a Node Project

Thanks to the popularity of Node, it's become the norm for every JavaScript project —whether intended for the browser, a Node server, or somewhere else—to start the same way: with a package.json. This file contains all the information about our project that Node might be interested in (such as the entry point module) as well as several pieces of human-oriented metadata (the description, author, license, and so on). Most importantly for our purposes, npm uses package.json to track dependencies like Jest.

---

2. https://github.com/getify/You-Dont-Know-JS
3. https://nodejs.org
4. https://cbednarski.com/articles/understanding-environment-variables-and-the-unix-path

Your first project will be called "test-driven-fizzbuzz." Create a directory with that name and cd into it:

```
$ mkdir test-driven-fizzbuzz
$ cd test-driven-fizzbuzz/
```

Create a package.json with all of the defaults by running npm init -y:

```
$ npm init -y
Wrote to ~/code/test-driven-fizzbuzz/package.json:

{
  "name": "test-driven-fizzbuzz",
  "version": "1.0.0",
  "description": "",
  "main": "index.js",
  "scripts": {
    "test": "echo \"Error: no test specified\" && exit 1"
  },
  "keywords": [],
  "author": "",
  "license": "ISC"
}
```

You'll want to make one tweak to the generated package.json. Assuming you don't plan on publishing this project to the npm registry, add the entry "private": true. You can do this on the command line with the npm pkg set command:

```
$ npm pkg set private=true
```

```
// package.json
{
  "name": "test-driven-fizzbuzz",
  "version": "1.0.0",
  "description": "",
  "main": "index.js",
  "scripts": {
    "test": "echo \"Error: no test specified\" && exit 1"
  },
  "keywords": [],
  "author": "",
  "license": "ISC",
  "private": "true"
}
```

The private flag prevents accidental publication and silences several npm warnings about our package not being publication-ready. It's a good practice to declare all new Node projects as private, then remove the private flag if and when you decide to publish.

Adding Jest as a Dependency

Use npm to install the jest package:

```
$ npm install --save-dev jest@29.4.3
...
npm created a lockfile as package-lock.json. You should commit this file.

+ jest@29.4.3
added 278 packages, and audited 279 packages in 8s

30 packages are looking for funding
  run `npm fund` for details
```

❶ The --save-dev flag tells npm, "I want to use the jest package for development only. My project doesn't need it at runtime." The jest@29.4.3 means "I want version 29.4.3 of the jest package."

❷ The information in package.json isn't enough for two machines to be guaranteed to get the same node_modules—even if you specify exact versions for all dependencies, you may get different versions of indirect dependencies. That's why npm creates a lockfile. If you're curious about the details, check out the npm docs.[5]

❸ The "178 packages" figure is striking, but it's normal for Node packages; you depend on one package, which depends on several other packages, which each in turn depend on several more, and so on. npm recursively installs all of them! If you're curious to see what all these packages are, take a peek at the freshly created node_modules directory.

❹ As JavaScript developers, we rely on open source software every day, much of it generously maintained by individuals in their free time. The npm fund command shows you projects in your dependency tree that are accepting donations. It's a great way to express your appreciation and support the JavaScript ecosystem!

If you open up package.json again, you'll see that npm has created a new entry called devDependencies:

```
// package.json
{
  ...
  "devDependencies": {
    "jest": "^29.4.3"
  }
}
```

---

5.   https://docs.npmjs.com/files/package-locks

That entry tells npm that the project depends on jest, but only in development. It also specifies a version range.

What Does the Caret (^) Before Version Numbers Mean?

By default, npm lists dependencies in package.json with a caret (^). The caret creates a version range that allows for minor updates and patches. So, jest@^29.4.3 includes any version of jest from version 29.4.3 up to, but not including, 30.0.0. According to semver principles, newer versions in that range should be backward compatible because package authors should bump the major version when making any breaking change. But be warned—package authors often ignore semver principles!

Fortunately, the other file npm created, package-lock.json, stores the exact version that was installed. As long as that lockfile is preserved, anyone who installs the project will get the exact same version of jest that you did. Put another way, npm install gives package-lock.json precedence over package.json. To install the latest version allowed by package.json, use the npm update command.

Now Jest is installed and ready for you to use. However, it's in the project's node_modules, not on your PATH. To run it, you'll need to call on another tool—npx.

Running Package Binaries with npx

In 2017, the npm team introduced a sibling project: npx.[6] Whereas npm is a package manager, npx is a package *runner*. Among other things, npx lets you run binaries from local Node packages without adding them to your PATH.

Try running Jest with the npx command:

```
$ npx jest
No tests found, exiting with code 1
Run with `--passWithNoTests` to exit with code 0
In /Users/tburnham/code/test-driven-fizzbuzz
  2 files checked.
  testMatch: **/__tests__/**/*.[jt]s?(x),
    **/?(*.)+(spec|test).[tj]s?(x) - 0 matches
  testPathIgnorePatterns: /node_modules/ - 2 matches
  testRegex:  - 0 matches
Pattern:  - 0 matches
```

Under the hood, npx jest is simply calling node_modules/.bin/jest. Check out the node_modules/.bin directory to see what other binaries are available from the packages in your dependency tree.

---

6. https://blog.npmjs.org/post/162869356040/introducing-npx-an-npm-package-runner

Any extra arguments you provide are passed to the binary that's being run with npx:

```
$ npx jest --version
29.4.3
```

If you use npx to try to run a command that isn't in your node_modules/.bin, it'll look up the package with that name and offer to install it for you (separately from your project's dependency tree). This is a powerful feature that we'll take advantage of in the next chapter.

You'll find that npx is an essential addition to your toolbelt! To learn more, read the npx docs.[7]

Running Project Scripts with npm

While npx provides a convenient solution for running binaries from your dependencies, it can also be useful to document the most commonly used commands in your project. The best way to do that is to list those commands in the scripts section of your project's package.json.

Scripts listed in scripts can be executed with npm run <script>. That command spawns a shell process that includes node_modules/.bin in its PATH, making npx unnecessary.

You may have noticed npm init put a placeholder test script in your package.json. Replace that script's contents with jest to produce the final package.json for this chapter:

```
ch1/package.json
{
  "name": "test-driven-fizzbuzz",
  "version": "1.0.0",
  "description": "",
  "main": "index.js",
  "scripts": {
    "test": "jest"
  },
  "keywords": [],
  "author": "",
  "license": "ISC",
  "private": "true",
  "devDependencies": {
    "jest": "^29.4.3"
  }
}
```

---

7.   https://docs.npmjs.com/cli/v9/commands/npx

The test script is special to npm; you can execute it with either npm run test or just npm test. You should see the same output that you got with npx jest:

```
$ npm test
No tests found, exiting with code 1
...
```

In Chapter 6, Continuous Integration and Collaboration, on page 123, you'll learn how to run your project scripts in the cloud.

Writing a Test

Time for your first test! Create a file called greeting.test.js:

```
// greeting.test.js
const greeting = guest => `Hello, ${guest}!`;
describe('greeting()', () => {
  it('says hello', () => {
    expect(greeting('Jest')).toBe('Hello, Jest!');
  });
});
```

❶ describe() declares a *test suite*, which is a grouping of tests. Its first argument is a name, and the second is a function containing one or more tests.

❷ it() declares a *test*. Its first argument is a name, and the second is a function with the actual test code.

❸ expect() creates an *assertion*. It takes a single argument, typically a value generated by the code being tested, and returns an object that provides a set of matcher functions.

toBe() is a *matcher* that performs a strict equality test between the value being tested (the expect() argument) and the expected value (its own argument).

Note the grammatical convention here: the test suite name ("greeting()") is a noun, and the test name ("says hello") is a verb. Together, they form a complete sentence describing the functionality covered by the test ("greeting() says hello"). This convention helps make test output easy to read. You can learn more about all of these methods in the Jest API docs.[8]

To run the test, all you need to do is invoke the jest CLI. By default, it finds and runs every file in the current project with the .test.js extension. Since you set jest as the test script in package.json, you can run it with npm run test:

---

8.   https://jestjs.io/docs/en/api

```
$ npm test
 PASS   ./greeting.test.js
  greeting()
    ✓ says hello (1 ms)

Test Suites: 1 passed, 1 total
Tests:       1 passed, 1 total
Snapshots:   0 total
Time:        0.159 s
Ran all test suites.
```

Excellent! Jest found the test file, ran the test, and confirmed that greeting('Jest') produces the string 'Hello, Jest!'.

You can go ahead and delete greeting.test.js:

```
$ rm greeting.test.js
```

In the next section, we'll start building this chapter's project.

The Tao of Test-Driven Development

Test-driven development (TDD) is sometimes defined as writing tests first. Although that's an important part of the methodology, it's not the essence. The essence of TDD is rapid iteration. You'll find that you learn more quickly from iterating—writing small, easy-to-understand pieces of code one at a time—than you would from trying to plan out a complex program from the ground up. You'll discover bad assumptions and potential pitfalls before you invest too much work. And you'll find the process more enjoyable, a smooth incremental progression rather than an alternation between bursts of inspiration and plateaus of "What do I do next?"

Our project for this chapter will be a solver for the classic programming challenge Fizz Buzz.[9] Here are the rules of Fizz Buzz:

> Write a program that prints the numbers from 1 to 100. But for multiples of three print "Fizz" instead of the number and for the multiples of five print "Buzz". For numbers which are multiples of both three and five print "FizzBuzz".

If that sounds simple to you, congratulations—you're a programmer!

In this section, you'll apply the TDD process to implementing a function that takes a number and returns the appropriate Fizz Buzz output. First, you'll write a single test, knowing that it'll fail. Second, you'll write an implementation that satisfies the test. Once the test is passing, you'll use Git to save your progress.

---

9.   http://wiki.c2.com/?FizzBuzzTest

Starting from Failure

Create an index.js with a placeholder implementation of fizzBuzz() so that your tests will have a valid referent:

```
// index.js
module.exports = (num) => `${num}`;
```

Now add an index.test.js with a test for a single Fizz Buzz rule:

```
// index.test.js
const fizzBuzz = require('./index');

describe('fizzBuzz()', () => {
  it('returns "FizzBuzz" for multiples of 3 and 5', () => {
    expect(fizzBuzz(15)).toBe('FizzBuzz');
    expect(fizzBuzz(30)).toBe('FizzBuzz');
  });
});
```

Run the test:

```
$ npm test
 FAIL  ./index.test.js
  fizzBuzz()
    ✕ returns "FizzBuzz" for multiples of 3 and 5 (2 ms)

  ● fizzBuzz() › returns "FizzBuzz" for multiples of 3 and 5

    expect(received).toBe(expected) // Object.is equality

    Expected: "FizzBuzz"
    Received: "15"

      3 | describe('fizzBuzz()', () => {
      4 |   it('returns "FizzBuzz" for multiples of 3 and 5', () => {
    > 5 |     expect(fizzBuzz(15)).toBe('FizzBuzz');
        |                          ^
      6 |     expect(fizzBuzz(30)).toBe('FizzBuzz');
      7 |   });
      8 | });

      at Object.toBe (index.test.js:5:26)

Test Suites: 1 failed, 1 total
Tests:       1 failed, 1 total
Snapshots:   0 total
Time:        0.178 s
Ran all test suites.
```

You may have cringed when you saw that glowing red FAIL. After all, having tests fail against production code is bad. But having tests fail during development can be a good thing! It means that you've anticipated some way your code *could* fail. Think of every failing test you see during development as a potential bug you've got a chance to preemptively squash.

Running Jest Tests Automatically

Jumping to the console every time you want to run some tests is a chore. Happily, Jest has a *watch mode* in which it automatically reruns all tests when it detects any change to a test file or to a source file depended on by a test.

To start Jest in watch mode, run it with the --watchAll flag:

```
$ npx jest --watchAll
```

Now you should see the same failure result as before. Try saving either index.js or index.test.js, and the test will rerun. (Blink and you might miss it!) You can press q at any time to quit. For now, leave Jest watch mode running.

Getting to Green

Since Jest is watching your project, see if you can tackle the "FizzBuzz" test case:

```
// index.js
module.exports = (num) => {
  if (num % 15 === 0) return 'FizzBuzz';
  return `${num}`
};
```

As soon as you hit save, your console output should change:

```
 PASS  ./index.test.js
  fizzBuzz()
    ✓ returns "FizzBuzz" for multiples of 3 and 5 (1 ms)

Test Suites: 1 passed, 1 total
Tests:       1 passed, 1 total
Snapshots:   0 total
Time:        0.114 s, estimated 1 s
Ran all test suites.
```

Achievement unlocked—you've just completed a test-driven development cycle!

Measuring Test Coverage

A great feature of Jest is its built-in code coverage measurement. This shows you how much of the code being tested actually ran during tests. To compute code coverage, add the --coverage flag:

```
$ npx jest --coverage
PASS  ./index.test.js
  fizzBuzz()
    ✓ returns "FizzBuzz" for multiples of 3 and 5 (1 ms)

----------|---------|----------|---------|---------|-------------------
File      | % Stmts | % Branch | % Funcs | % Lines | Uncovered Line #s
----------|---------|----------|---------|---------|-------------------
All files |      75 |       50 |     100 |   66.66 |
 index.js |      75 |       50 |     100 |   66.66 | 3
----------|---------|----------|---------|---------|-------------------
Test Suites: 1 passed, 1 total
Tests:       1 passed, 1 total
Snapshots:   0 total
Time:        0.133 s, estimated 1 s
Ran all test suites.
```

Here the report shows 75% of statements were covered, and 50% of branches. "Branches" refer to the possible outcomes of if/else statements. The 50% result reflects the fact that the current test only covers the case where the condition num % 15 === 0 passes. Try adding a test to cover the case where it fails:

```
// index.test.js
const fizzBuzz = require('../index');

describe('fizzBuzz()', () => {
  it('returns "FizzBuzz" for multiples of 3 and 5', () => {
    expect(fizzBuzz(15)).toBe('FizzBuzz');
    expect(fizzBuzz(30)).toBe('FizzBuzz');
  });

  it('returns the given number for multiples of neither 3 nor 5', () => {
    expect(fizzBuzz(1)).toBe('1');
    expect(fizzBuzz(22)).toBe('22');
  });
});
```

Then run the test with code coverage again:

```
$ npx jest --coverage
 PASS  ./index.test.js
  fizzBuzz()
    ✓ returns "FizzBuzz" for multiples of 3 and 5 (1 ms)
    ✓ returns the given number for multiples of neither 3 nor 5
```

```
----------|---------|----------|---------|---------|-------------------
File      | % Stmts | % Branch | % Funcs | % Lines | Uncovered Line #s
----------|---------|----------|---------|---------|-------------------
All files |     100 |      100 |     100 |     100 |
 index.js |     100 |      100 |     100 |     100 |
----------|---------|----------|---------|---------|-------------------
Test Suites: 1 passed, 1 total
Tests:       2 passed, 2 total
Snapshots:   0 total
Time:        0.153 s, estimated 1 s
Ran all test suites.
```

Perfect! The report confirms that every possible code path was taken when the tests ran.

Like all metrics, code coverage is imperfect—projects with impressive code coverage numbers don't necessarily have the most *useful* tests—but the numbers can still guide you in the right direction. It's especially handy for identifying parts of your project with large gaps in test coverage.

Checking in Changes

Whenever you add a new test and get it to pass, that's a good time to get your project into source control. That way, no matter what you do to the project, you can always restore it to the all-green state later.

We'll use Git as our source control system in this book. If you're not familiar with Git, you might want to read through the "Git Basics" section of the excellent (and free) *Pro Git* by Scott Chacon and Ben Straub.[10]

The first step is initializing this project as a Git repository:

```
$ git init
Initialized empty Git repository in
/Users/tburnham/code/test-driven-fizzbuzz/.git/
```

Don't commit just yet. Although your project is brand new, there are a *staggering* number of files in it! Remember those "178 packages" npm mentioned when you installed Jest? They're all hanging out in the project's node_modules directory. Fortunately, we don't need to keep them in source control, because all of the information needed to re-create the node_modules tree is contained in package-lock.json. So tell Git to ignore the installed packages by creating a .gitignore file at the root of the project:

ch1/.gitignore
```
node_modules/
```

---

10. https://git-scm.com/book/en/v2/Git-Basics-Getting-a-Git-Repository#ch02-git-basics-chapter

There. Now the project looks a lot more manageable, from Git's point of view:

```
$ git status
On branch main

No commits yet

Untracked files:
  (use "git add <file>..." to include in what will be committed)
        .gitignore
        index.js
        index.test.js
        package-lock.json
        package.json

nothing added to commit but untracked files present (use "git add" to track)
```

All of those files belong in source control, so stage them for commit:

```
$ git add .
```

Just for fun, this book uses gitmoji[11] for all of its commit messages. These are ASCII-friendly aliases that render as emoji on GitHub and in some other tools. For a project's first commit, the appropriate gitmoji is :tada:, which represents the Party Popper emoji:[12]

```
$ git commit -m ":tada: First commit"
[main (root-commit) dca2255] :tada: First commit
 5 files changed, 5893 insertions(+)
 create mode 100644 .gitignore
 create mode 100644 index.js
 create mode 100644 index.test.js
 create mode 100644 package-lock.json
 create mode 100644 package.json
```

Congrats on completing your first feature! You wrote a test for the feature, made the test pass, and then checked that change into source control. Satisfying, isn't it?

As an exercise, see if you can repeat the TDD process for the remaining Fizz Buzz requirements. Namely, your fizzBuzz() function should return the following:

1. "Fizz" for multiples of 3
2. "Buzz" for multiples of 5
3. The given number for multiples of neither 3 nor 5

---

11. https://gitmoji.carloscuesta.me
12. https://emojipedia.org/party-popper/

For each of those requirements, add a test within the same suite (the `describe()` block), modify the implementation to make everything pass, then move to the next requirement. You can find an example solution at the end of the chapter.

Mantra: Red, Green, Repeat

Each chapter of this book concludes with a mantra, a phrase you can repeat to yourself to bring clarity whenever you're feeling unfocused. This chapter's mantra—*Red, green, repeat*—encapsulates test-driven development (TDD) in a nutshell. In the long term, the habit of putting tests first helps to form a healthy mindset for problem solving, one in which failing code evokes curiosity instead of despair.

In the abstract, the act of writing tests before code may seem inconsequential. Writing code and writing tests are, one might imagine, two activities that can be done in any order with identical results. But imagining is one thing; hands-on experience is another. If you've done the exercise for this chapter, and taken advantage of Jest's watch mode, then you know the feeling of satisfaction at watching a test flip from red to green as your code clicks into place.

And it doesn't have to stop there. With the new code still fresh in your mind, you can experiment. Try a different approach. Use cleaner syntax. Refactor. As soon as you save, the test console will tell you if your revision is viable. With just a few extra minutes, you can almost always find a way to make your code better. More importantly, what you learn from these little ventures will make you a better coder.

The entire TDD methodology is made possible by rapid feedback. But tests aren't the only possible source of that feedback. In the next chapter, you'll get to know TypeScript and ESLint, two automated checkers that can help you identify potential errors. And you'll find out how you can integrate feedback from those tools directly into VS Code.

Example Fizz Buzz Solution

ch1/index.test.js
```js
const fizzBuzz = require('./index');

describe('fizzBuzz()', () => {
  it('returns "FizzBuzz" for multiples of 3 and 5', () => {
    expect(fizzBuzz(15)).toBe('FizzBuzz');
    expect(fizzBuzz(30)).toBe('FizzBuzz');
  });

  it('returns "Fizz" for multiples of 3', () => {
    expect(fizzBuzz(3)).toBe('Fizz');
    expect(fizzBuzz(33)).toBe('Fizz');
  });

  it('returns "Buzz" for multiples of 5', () => {
    expect(fizzBuzz(5)).toBe('Buzz');
    expect(fizzBuzz(20)).toBe('Buzz');
  });

  it('returns the given number for multiples of neither 3 nor 5', () => {
    expect(fizzBuzz(1)).toBe('1');
    expect(fizzBuzz(22)).toBe('22');
  });
});
```

ch1/index.js
```js
module.exports = (num) => {
  if (num % 15 === 0) return 'FizzBuzz';
  if (num % 3 === 0) return 'Fizz';
  if (num % 5 === 0) return 'Buzz';
  return `${num}`
};
```

CHAPTER 2

Integrated Tooling with VS Code

As we learned in the previous chapter, the essence of test-driven development is rapid iteration. Instead of waiting until you've churned out a whole feature before finding out if your code works, you split that feature into small pieces and enjoy feedback as you put each piece in place.

Ideally, the kind of feedback used for TDD should be automated (no effort required) and fast (no waiting). We've seen how helpful Jest's watch mode is in both regards. But you can do even better by incorporating feedback directly into your code editing environment.

This chapter is about that environment. It starts with VS Code, a powerful and highly customizable editor. Later in the chapter, you'll incorporate some new tools into this coding environment: TypeScript (which checks that variables are used in a way that makes sense for their type), ESLint (which detects common mistakes and code style issues), and Prettier (which autoformats code so you can stay focused on substance over style). Last but not least, you'll experience Wallaby, a magical piece of software that bridges the gap between your code and your tests to give you real-time feedback.

The goal is to get you acquainted with all of the pieces of a modern JavaScript development stack. Although this chapter is a bit of a detour, you'll find the arsenal of support tools introduced here invaluable when you take on the challenge of React development, starting in Chapter 3, Testing React with Testing Library, on page 45.

If you're already comfortable with your development environment, feel free to skim this chapter. The aim here isn't to convince you to switch to VS Code but rather to minimize the friction between you and your tools by setting them up to silently watch over your code. If you need to run a command every time you want to see if your tests are passing, your process has too much friction!

Editing with VS Code

Microsoft's Visual Studio Code (VS Code for short) is a relatively new entry in the world of code editors. First launched in 2015, it rapidly rose to become the most popular editor in the JavaScript community. What makes VS Code special is its incredible extensibility. A rich ecosystem of VS Code extensions is available, especially for JavaScript development, as we'll soon see.

> ## Visual Studio vs. VS Code
>
> Don't confuse Visual Studio Code with Visual Studio. The two are about as similar as JavaScript and Java, another oddly co-branded pair. Whereas Visual Studio is an enterprise-grade commercial IDE made for Windows, VS Code is a sleek, cross-platform text editor inspired by Sublime Text and Atom. It's also completely open source.[a]
>
> _____
>
> a.   https://github.com/microsoft/vscode

In this section, we'll get to know VS Code as we use it to start a new test-driven JavaScript project.

Launching VS Code and the Integrated Terminal

To get started, download and install the latest VS Code release.[1] Open it up and take a look around. We'll only cover the essentials of the editor in this book; for more details on everything you're looking at, see the User Interface[2] page in the official docs.

The most important feature to know about in VS Code is the *Command Palette*, as shown in the screenshot on page 19.

The Command Palette is a single searchable list of every command that VS Code supports. Anytime you hear a command referenced by name, you can find and execute it from the Command Palette. To open the Command Palette, type ⇧⌘P (macOS) or ⇧^P (Windows and Linux).

_____

1.   https://code.visualstudio.com
2.   https://code.visualstudio.com/docs/getstarted/userinterface

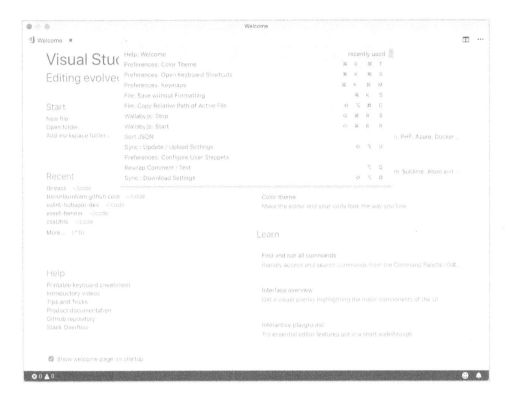

If another editor's built-in keyboard shortcuts are ingrained in your muscle memory, you can make the transition to VS Code easier by installing a keymap. Keymaps, a type of VS Code extension, add key bindings. From the Command Palette, select Preferences: Keymaps. A list of all available keymaps will appear in the sidebar. Click the Install button for the one corresponding to your favorite (for now) editor, then click the blue Restart button that replaces it. Now those familiar keyboard shortcuts are at your ready.

If you're on macOS, you should run one other VS Code command right away: "Shell Command: Install code command in PATH." The code utility lets you open files and directories in VS Code from the command line. If you're on Windows or Linux, code should have already been installed for you.

Now take another look around. Most of the workspace is occupied by the editor area. By default, that area is occupied by a Welcome page. Close that tab. With no files open, the editor area shows a handy list of commonly used keyboard shortcuts, as you can see in the screenshot on page 20.

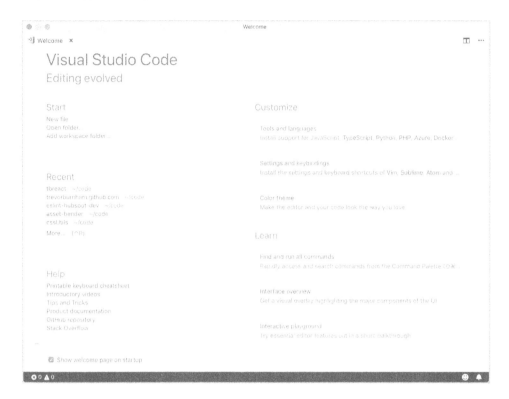

Try one of those now: Toggle Terminal (^`). A shell will pop up from the bottom of the screen. For any developer used to switching back and forth between their editor and their terminal, this integrated terminal is a game-changer. Try using it to create the directory for this chapter's project, test-driven-palindromes:

```
$ mkdir test-driven-palindromes
```

Then open that directory using the code command-line utility. By default, code [dir] opens dir in a new window; since we don't need our existing workspace, add the -r flag (short for --reuse-window):

```
$ code -r test-driven-palindromes
```

Now VS Code knows that you're working on a project in the test-driven-palindromes directory, which lets the editor help you out in a number of ways. For a start, every Terminal instance now opens with test-driven-palindromes as its working directory. Try it:

```
$ pwd
/Users/tburnham/code/test-driven-palindromes
```

Let's start building our new project. The first file we'll need is a package.json. Use npm init -y again to create one with all of the defaults:

```
$ npm init -y
Wrote to /Users/trevor.burnham/code/test-driven-palindromes/package.json:

{
  "name": "test-driven-palindromes",
  "version": "1.0.0",
  "description": "",
  "main": "index.js",
  "scripts": {
    "test": "echo \"Error: no test specified\" && exit 1"
  },
  "keywords": [],
  "author": "",
  "license": "ISC"
}
```

Add "private": true to prevent the package from being accidentally published:

```
$ npm pkg set private=true
```

Now install Jest along with its companion type definitions @types/jest—those types will come in handy later in the chapter:

```
$ npm install --save-dev jest@29.4.3 @types/jest@29.4.0
```

Open the new package.json in the editor by clicking it in the Explorer sidebar or by using the handy Go to File command (⌘P on macOS, ^P on Windows and Linux) to search for it. Then replace the boilerplate "test" script with "jest", as in the previous chapter:

```
// package.json
{
  "name": "test-driven-palindromes",
  "version": "1.0.0",
  "description": "",
  "main": "index.js",
  "scripts": {
➤    "test": "jest"
  },
  "keywords": [],
  "author": "",
  "license": "ISC",
  "private": "true",
  "devDependencies": {
    "jest": "^29.4.3",
    "@types/jest": "^29.4.0",
  }
}
```

Then toggle the terminal again (^`) to get it out of the way. You won't need it for the next section.

Using Editor Groups

Let's get back into the rhythm of TDD. For our project, we're going to write a function that finds all palindromes in a string. A palindrome is a phrase that's spelled the same forward and backward (ignoring spaces and punctuation). For example, take a look at the following:

```
palindromes('What number is never odd or even, asked the Sphinx?')
```

It would return this:

```
['neveroddoreven']
```

As frivolous as a program for finding palindromes may sound, it's a good approximation of a real project in one important sense: the requirements aren't precisely defined. Whereas Fizz Buzz had crystal-clear rules that we could translate directly into tests, figuring out a reasonable set of rules for the palindrome finder will require creativity and experimentation.

Create a New Untitled File (⌘N on macOS, ^N on Windows and Linux), then save it (⌘S on macOS, ^S on Windows and Linux) as palindromes.js. Repeat for palindromes.test.js.

Now let's try viewing the two files side-by-side: palindromes.js on the left, palindromes.test.js on the right. You can do this in several ways. If you're a mouse person, the fastest way is to click-and-drag the palindromes.test.js tab to the right edge of the editor area. If you'd rather stick with the keyboard, trigger the Move Editor into Right Group command from the Command Palette.

Now all the relevant parts of the project are in view. You can move the focus to different editor groups by pressing the primary modifier key (⌘ on macOS, ^ on Windows and Linux) with the number corresponding to the group's ordinal position. So palindromes.js is ⌘1 or ^1, and palindromes.test.js is ⌘2 or ^2. This even works from the Terminal.

In palindromes.test.js, create the first test:

```
// palindromes.test.js
const palindromes = require('./palindromes')

describe('palindromes()', () => {
  it('correctly identifies one-word palindromes', () => {
    expect(palindromes('madam')).toEqual(['madam']);
  });
});
```

❶ Previously, we've made equality assertions with toBe(). However, toBe() does a strict equality check (like the === operator), which would fail here. The toEqual() assertion method, by contrast, checks for deep object equality. So the assertion expect(x).toEqual(['madam']) passes as long as x is an array with the string "madam" as its only entry.

In palindromes.js, write a placeholder implementation:

```
// palindromes.js
module.exports = (str) => {
  return [str];
};
```

Then open the integrated Terminal and start Jest in watch mode:

```
$ npx jest --watchAll
```

The resulting layout should resemble the following screenshot, with your code and test output visible all at once:

The test should light up green. Time to check your work in! In the next section, we'll see how VS Code streamlines common Git tasks.

Integrated Source Control

VS Code features superb Git integration right out of the box. Stage changes, make commits, view diffs, switch branches, push to remotes—you can do it all without even opening the Terminal. Try opening the Command Palette and typing "git" to get a sense of all the power at your disposal.

Before you initialize Git for your new project, you'll need to do some preemptive ignoring. That node_modules directory is going to gum up the works if you let it! So create a .gitignore file, just like the one in the previous chapter's project:

```
# .gitignore
node_modules/
```

Now use the Command Palette to run Git: Initialize Repository. When you're prompted to choose a directory, accept the default. This is equivalent to running git init from the command line in the project directory.

With Git initialized, the branch icon on the left edge of the window comes to life, showing a badge with the number 5. This is the number of files with uncommitted changes (which, since we have no commits yet, is all non-ignored files). Click that icon or press ⌃⇧G to open the Source Control sidebar, as shown in the following screenshot:

The Source Control sidebar shows you a list of modified files. You can click any of the file names to see a diff view, showing exactly what changes you can stage for commit. You could hover each of the files and click the + icon to stage it, but since you want to stage and commit everything, there's a faster way. Type this commit message into the Message box above the list of changes:

```
:tada: First commit
```

Confirm the commit by pressing ⌘↵ (macOS) or ^↵ (Windows and Linux). You'll get a prompt asking if you'd like for VS Code to automatically stage all your changes before committing. Select Always. This will write an entry in your User Settings, which is the subject of the next subsection.

User Settings

A code editor is only as good as a developer's ability to tailor it to their needs. The VS Code team, knowing this, designed for customizability. All user-level customizations live in a single, editable JSON file, with the exception of keyboard shortcuts, which have their own dedicated customization file.

Recent versions of VS Code added a friendly, graphical settings interface. However, it's useful to see what lurks underneath. From the Command Palette, run Preferences: Open Settings (JSON). This opens up a JSON file with all of your personal setting overrides. Since this view doesn't show you the default setting, though, it's not very useful by itself. You can remedy that by adding this setting:

```
"workbench.settings.useSplitJSON": true
```

Save the file and reopen the settings file. Now you'll be taken to a split view, with VS Code's default settings on the left and your user-level overrides on the right, as shown in the screenshot on page 26.

If you chose Always at the Git commit prompt in the last section, then there will be one other override here: git.enableSmartCommit is set to true. Hovering over the rule's name gives you a description of its meaning:

```
Commit all changes when there are no staged changes.
```

If you'd like to change the look and feel of the editor, now's your chance! Let's say you want to change the font. Type "font" in the search bar, and you'll see several matching settings. Hover over any of the matches and click the pencil icon to copy that setting over to your User Settings, where you can do with it what you like. For example, if 12px is a bit squint-inducing for you, you

might copy editor.fontSize to your User Settings and change the value to 14. As soon as you save, the change will take effect, as shown in the screenshot on page 27.

You can also change the color theme (used for both UI and syntax highlighting) via the workbench.colorTheme setting. However, a useful shortcut is to use the Color Theme command, accessible from the context menu on the gear in the lower-left corner. You'll be presented with a list of every installed theme. You can preview them by using ↑ and ↓ to highlight each one.

If none of the themes included with VS Code suit you, you can find many more in the VS Code marketplace.[3]

Aside from typography and color choice, perhaps nothing provokes as much developer passion as shells, at least among us Mac devotees. If you want to make the integrated Terminal launch something other than the version of Bash that came with the OS, override the terminal.integrated.shell.osx setting to point to your favorite shell.

---

3.   https://marketplace.visualstudio.com/vscode

One more setting of note—you've probably noticed the smiley face in the lower-right corner, soliciting feedback for the VS Code team. Many developers find it annoying. If you're one of them, just right-click it and select Hide from the context menu. This'll add an override for the workbench.statusBar.feedback.visible setting:

```
// User Settings
{
    "git.enableSmartCommit": true,
    "workbench.settings.useSplitJSON": true,
    "workbench.statusBar.feedback.visible": false,
}
```

Once you have VS Code adjusted to your liking, we'll make some project-level tweaks.

Workspace Settings

Sometimes you'll want to change an editor setting for a particular project. In VS Code, this feature is called Workspace Settings. Entries in Workspace Settings take precedence over User Settings.

Next to the User Settings heading above the right editor pane, you'll notice a Workspace Settings heading. Click it. As soon as you do, a new file will materialize in the project: .vscode/settings.json. You add overrides to this file the same way that you do with User Settings.

One good use of Workspace Settings is telling VS Code to ignore non-editable files that live in the project via the files.exclude setting. For our purposes, the node_modules directory and package-lock.json are both non-editable, since we want npm to manage them for us:

```
// .vscode/settings.json
{
    "files.exclude": {
        "node_modules": true,
        "package-lock.json": true
    }
}
```

❶ Object settings like this one don't replace the default; instead, the two objects are merged. To remove a key from the default files.exclude. object, copy its key and set the value to false.

Open the Explorer sidebar. You'll notice that node_modules and package-lock.json are gone. They'll also be excluded from all searches, including Go to File (though node_modules was already excluded from searches, thanks to the default search.exclude setting). It's worth emphasizing that files.exclude and .gitignore are completely independent: Git will continue to monitor package-lock.json, which means that changes to that file will continue to be listed in the Source Control sidebar.

Another good use of Workspace Settings is indentation. VS Code defaults to using four-space indentation when it can't automatically detect the existing indentation level of a file. Since this book uses two-space indentation for all JavaScript code, try adding a Workspace Setting that stipulates two-space indentation only within JavaScript files:

```
// .vscode/settings.json
{
    "files.exclude": {
        "node_modules": true,
        "package-lock.json": true
    },
    "[javascript]": {
        "editor.tabSize": 2
    }
}
```

❶ The [javascript] key tells VS Code, "Apply all settings within this block only to JavaScript files."

In general, the Workspace Settings file shouldn't be checked into source control, since individual contributors to the same project may want different project-level customizations. So open .gitignore and add the .vscode directory:

```
ch2/.gitignore
node_modules/
.vscode/
```

Now switch to the Source Control sidebar and commit, using the gitmoji for .gitignore changes:

```
:see_no_evil: Ignore .vscode dir
```

This concludes our whirlwind tour of VS Code's most essential features. You've learned how to use the super-convenient integrated terminal and source control, how to jump to files without touching the mouse, and how to open editors in a side-by-side split view. Most importantly, you realized the power to adjust every little detail of the editor to your liking through User Settings and Workspace Settings.

In the rest of the chapter, you'll go beyond the out-of-the-box capabilities of VS Code by adding extensions specifically tailored for a refined JavaScript development experience.

Checking Code Quality with ESLint

A linter is a program that uses a set of rules to detect code that, though syntactically valid, is likely to contain mistakes. A classic example is using = (assignment) instead of == or === (equality) in an if statement:

```
if (savings = 0) {
  // This "condition" would empty your bank account!
}
```

Linting JavaScript is especially valuable because of its relatively freewheeling nature. If you mistype window as wimdow, your program won't refuse to run; it just won't run the way you'd hoped. Of course, one way to avoid such fat-finger bugs is to have extensive test coverage. But a linter can often identify such problems sooner and give you more helpful information for fixing them. Enter ESLint.[4]

---

4.   https://eslint.org/

Although other JavaScript linters have been tried before, ESLint is the first to really take off, thanks to its pluggable architecture. Plugins are available for React, Angular, and every other popular JavaScript framework, aimed at warning developers against the most common gotchas. And what do you know—there's a Jest plugin too!

You'll find that linting is an invaluable addition to your TDD toolbelt—one that you'll continue to use throughout this book. In this section, you'll learn how to run ESLint, how to configure it, and how to integrate it with VS Code for fast, automatic feedback.

Installing and Configuring ESLint

Let's add ESLint to our project. First, open the VS Code Terminal. If Jest is running in watch mode, press Q to quit. Then install the eslint package along with its companion type definitions, @types/eslint:

```
$ npm install --save-dev eslint@8.35.0 @types/eslint@8.21.1
+ eslint@8.35.0
+ @types/eslint@8.21.1
```

You can try running ESLint with npx eslint, but it won't do anything yet—the project needs an ESLint configuration first. Create a new file and save it as .eslintrc.js:

```
// .eslintrc.js
❶ /** @type {import('eslint').Linter.Config} */
module.exports = {
❷   extends: ['eslint:recommended'],
};
```

❶ This JSDoc-style comment lets VS Code know what kind of object you're writing by referencing a type definition from the @types/eslint package. (By convention, the @types/ namespace is omitted, since many packages—but not ESLint—have their type definitions built in.) Although the editor won't stop you from writing an object that doesn't conform to the specified type, it will give you helpful suggestions. Try typing "" for one of the object keys to get a list of possible completions. Comments like this are a great way of bringing some of the benefits of TypeScript into config files that can't be written in TypeScript. We'll properly introduce TypeScript later in this chapter.

❷ extends allows an ESLint configuration to inherit properties from another ESLint configuration. You can view the eslint:recommended configuration in the ESLint source code.[5]

This tells ESLint to use its recommended rule set as the base for our configuration. For a complete list of the included rules, check the ESLint docs.[6] We'll tweak those rules in the next section. Try linting palindromes.js now:

```
$ npx eslint palindromes.js
/Users/tburnham/code/test-driven-palindromes/palindromes.js
  1:25  error  Parsing error: Unexpected token >

✖ 1 problem (1 error, 0 warnings)
```

ESLint refused to parse the arrow function syntax (expression) => { ... }. By default, ESLint makes the conservative assumption that all code must conform to the now-ancient ECMAScript 5 standard. Arrow functions were added in ECMAScript 6, aka ECMAScript 2015.

We're running our code under Node 18, which supports all features up to ECMAScript 2021.[7] Add a new entry to the ESLint configuration:

```
// .eslintrc.js
/** @type {import('eslint').Linter.Config} */
module.exports = {
  extends: ['eslint:recommended'],
  env: {
    es2021: true,
  }
};
```

Run the linter again, and you'll see a different error:

```
$ npx eslint palindromes.js
/Users/tburnham/code/test-driven-palindromes/palindromes.js
  1:1  error  'module' is not defined  no-undef

✖ 1 problem (1 error, 0 warnings)
```

Once again, ESLint is erring on the side of caution. The module global isn't part of any ECMAScript standard and would indeed be undefined in many environments. We expect it to be defined, however, because this code will run in a Node environment. To let ESLint know that, add another env entry:

---

5.   https://github.com/eslint/eslint/blob/main/packages/js/src/configs/eslint-recommended.js
6.   https://eslint.org/docs/rules/
7.   https://compat-table.github.io/compat-table/es2016plus

```
// .eslintrc.js
/** @type {import('eslint').Linter.Config} */
module.exports = {
  extends: ['eslint:recommended'],
  env: {
    node: true,
    es2021: true,
  },
};
```

Now give the linter one more try:

```
$ npx eslint palindromes.js
```

No output? Great! When it comes to linting, no news is good news.

Commit your work so far, using the gitmoji for configuration changes:

```
:wrench: Initial ESLint setup
```

If you'd like more information on anything we've done so far, see the docs on configuring ESLint.[8] Next up, we're going to build a slightly different set of linter rules for our test file.

Extending an ESLint Configuration

ESLint is now perfectly content with palindromes.js, but if you try to run it against palindromes.test.js, it won't be so happy:

```
$ npx eslint palindromes.test.js
/Users/tburnham/code/test-driven-palindromes/palindromes.test.js
  3:1  error  'describe' is not defined  no-undef
  4:3  error  'it' is not defined        no-undef
  5:5  error  'expect' is not defined    no-undef

✖ 3 problems (3 errors, 0 warnings)
```

All of these problems share the same cause as the module kerfuffle earlier: ESLint doesn't know that palindromes.test.js will be running in an environment (Jest) where describe, it, and expect are defined as globals.

You could fix the problem with another 'env' entry, but there's a better way. Jest has an official ESLint plugin, eslint-plugin-jest,[9] which comes with several rules for identifying common test code mistakes. Go ahead and add it to the project:

```
$ npm install --save-dev eslint-plugin-jest@27.2.1
+ eslint-plugin-jest@27.2.1
```

---

8. https://eslint.org/docs/user-guide/configuring
9. https://github.com/jest-community/eslint-plugin-jest

To apply the plugin, you need to make two changes to the ESLint configuration. First, register it in a plugins entry, and second, add its recommended configuration to the extends entry:

```
// .eslintrc.js
/** @type {import('eslint').Linter.Config} */
module.exports = {
➤   plugins: ['jest'],
➤   extends: ['eslint:recommended', 'plugin:jest/recommended'],
    env: {
      node: true,
      es2021: true,
    },
};
```

Now you should be able to lint palindromes.test.js without complaint:

```
$ npx eslint palindromes.test.js
```

However, we have a slight problem with this setup: those Jest-specific configuration settings now apply to every JavaScript file in the project! Ideally, we only want those settings to apply in test files.

We can accomplish that using an override block that applies certain settings only to *.test.js files:

```
// .eslintrc.js
/** @type {import('eslint').Linter.Config} */
module.exports = {
    extends: ['eslint:recommended'],
    env: {
      node: true,
      es2021: true,
    },
➤   overrides: [
➤     {
➤       files: ['*.test.js'],
➤       plugins: ['jest'],
➤       extends: ['plugin:jest/recommended'],
➤     },
➤   ],
};
```

Now when ESLint runs against palindromes.test.js, it'll apply both the base configuration from eslint:recommended and the additional configuration from plugin:jest/recommended.

Try it out for yourself:

```
$ npx eslint palindromes.test.js
```

Once you get the all-clear, commit the updated configuration:

```
:wrench: Add eslint-plugin-jest
```

Integrating ESLint with VS Code

As useful as ESLint's command-line reports are, they're less than ideal ergonomically. First, running the linter manually takes you out of your coding flow. And second, using the line and column numbers in the error report to identify the code in question is a chore. It'd be much handier to see the linter's feedback directly in your code. Happily, we can do exactly that by adding the ESLint extension to VS Code.

Open the Extensions sidebar (^⇧X) and search for "ESLint". Several extensions will pop up. At the top of the list, you should see an extension simply named ESLint.[10] Click the Install button.

Try typing something nonsensical in either of the project's JS files. Within milliseconds, your gibberish will be underlined in bright red. ESLint is linting your code as you type! Hover over the underlined code to see which linter rule you're breaking. Also notice that the scrollbar area (officially called the "overview ruler") has red squares marking the lines with red underlining—handy for scrolling directly to linter problems in large files.

VS Code tracks all problems reported by linters and aggregates them in the left corner of the status bar (next to the source control branch indicator), where you can always see the total number of errors and warnings found in all open files. Click these numbers and the Problems pane will open with a complete list, as you can see in the screenshot on page 35.

You can click any of the listed problems to jump to the corresponding point in your code. To get a feel for how all of this feedback can help, try adding another assertion to the existing test:

```
// palindromes.test.js
const palindromes = require('./palindromes');

describe('palindromes()', () => {
  it('correctly identifies one-word palindromes', () => {
    expect(palindromes('madam')).toEqual(['madam']);
    expect(palindromes('racecar')).toEqual(['racecar']);
  })
});
```

---

10. https://marketplace.visualstudio.com/items?itemName=dbaeumer.vscode-eslint

Any mistake you make will trigger instant alarm bells. If, for example, you were to misplace the closing parenthesis for the expect() so that it contained the toEqual(), the linter would complain (thanks to the Jest plugin) that No assertion was called on expect().

Having linter feedback as you type is terrific for catching typos, but it also means getting a lot of false positives, as the linter is liable to complain before you've finished typing what you've intended. Many developers don't mind this, but if you'd prefer to do without the noise, you can tell the ESLint integration to wait until save via the eslint.run setting:

```
// User Settings
{
    ...
    "eslint.run": "onSave",
}
```

And that's all you need to get up and running with ESLint. We've seen how to add ESLint to a project, how to use nested configurations, and how to run the linter automatically with VS Code. In the next section, we'll take our quest for better code through better tooling even further with automated formatting.

Beautifying Code with Prettier

Prettier[11] describes itself as "an opinionated code formatter." First introduced in 2017, it's already soared to two million downloads per week from the npm registry. Using Prettier for the first time feels like a breath of fresh air—no more worrying about insignificant stylistic details as you work. No more arguments with your team about what's most readable. Just let the formatter take care of it!

Let's add Prettier to the project:

```
$ npm install --save-dev prettier@2.8.4
+ prettier@2.8.4
```

Try running prettier against the test suite:

```
$ npx prettier palindromes.test.js
const palindromes = require("./palindromes");

describe("palindromes()", () => {
  it("correctly identifies one-word palindromes", () => {
    expect(palindromes("madam")).toEqual(["madam"]);
    expect(palindromes("racecar")).toEqual(["racecar"]);
  });
});
```

Prettier read palindromes.test.js and emitted a formatted version as its output. It didn't change the file itself, though you could do that by adding the --write flag to the command.

If you typed the original code exactly as it was presented in the book, there's only one change in the formatted version: the strings are double-quoted rather than single-quoted, per Prettier's default configuration.

Prettier is a famously opinionated tool. Whereas ESLint is infinitely customizable, Prettier offers only a handful of configuration options.[12] And it comes out of the box with defaults that have been carefully chosen to reflect popular norms for JavaScript development. We'll be sticking with those defaults throughout this book.

Even though we aren't setting any configuration options, it's best to add a Prettier configuration file to the project so that tooling will recognize that the project is Prettier-enabled:

```
ch2/.prettierrc.js
module.exports = {};
```

---

11. https://prettier.io/
12. https://prettier.io/docs/en/options.html

Preventing Conflicts Between ESLint and Prettier

We now have two tools set up to format files in our project: ESLint and Prettier. But what happens if they have different ideas about how a particular file should be formatted?

Rather than having the formatters duke it out, we can make them play nice by installing eslint-config-prettier,[13] which simply disables all ESLint rules that potentially conflict with Prettier's formatting:

```
$ npm install --save-dev eslint-config-prettier@8.7.0
+ eslint-config-prettier@8.7.0
```

Then add "prettier" to the extends list in the ESLint config:

```
ch2/.eslintrc.js
/** @type {import('eslint').Linter.Config} */
module.exports = {
  extends: ["eslint:recommended", "prettier"],
  env: {
    node: true,
    es2021: true,
  },
  overrides: [
    {
      files: ["*.test.js"],
      plugins: ["jest"],
      extends: ["plugin:jest/recommended"],
    },
  ],
};
```

Now the two tools can peacefully coexist! Open the Source Control sidebar and commit:

```
:wrench: Initial Prettier setup
```

Integrating Prettier with VS Code

As with ESLint, Prettier works best when integrated into your editor, allowing you to format your code with a single keystroke—or, if you prefer, without you even having to ask.

Open the Extensions sidebar (^⇧X) and search for Prettier. At the top of the list you should see the official Prettier extension.[14] Click the Install button.

---

13. https://github.com/prettier/eslint-config-prettier
14. https://marketplace.visualstudio.com/items?itemName=esbenp.prettier-vscode

Prettier is what's known as a *formatter extension*. When you run the Format Document command (⇧⌥F), VS Code checks the installed extensions to see if any of them wants to perform formatting on the given document. Open up, say, palindromes.test.js, and run that command now. The results should be exactly the same as if you ran npx prettier --write palindromes.test.js.

As handy as the Format Document command is, we can do better. Open the project's Workspace Settings and add one final customization, editor.formatOnSave:

ch2/.vscode/settings.json
```
{
  "files.exclude": {
    "node_modules": true,
    "package-lock.json": true
  },
  "[javascript]": {
    "editor.tabSize": 2
  },
  "editor.formatOnSave": true
}
```

The editor.formatOnSave flag does just what it sounds like, running Format Document for you every time you save a file. Try it now—open up a few files in the project, make tweaks, hit save, and watch them instantly change. Achieving consistent formatting has never been easier!

If you're feeling adventurous (or impatient), there's also an editor.formatOnType flag. Most developers find this mode too jarring, but if you have a taste for instant feedback, it's worth trying out.

Adding Project Lint Scripts

You've learned how to run ESLint and Prettier from the command line with npx and directly from your editor. But that knowledge is locked inside your head! To make your project more approachable to potential collaborators, it's a good idea to include some linting scripts in package.json.

Here we have a lint script that tests all JS files for lints and formatting issues, and a format script that runs all JS files through Prettier and overwrites the originals:

ch2/package.json
```
{
  "name": "test-driven-palindromes",
  "version": "1.0.0",
  "description": "",
  "main": "index.js",
  "scripts": {
    "test": "jest",
```

```
❶      "lint": "eslint . && prettier --list-different .",
❷      "format": "eslint --fix . && prettier --log-level warn --write ."
     },
     "keywords": [],
     "author": "",
     "license": "ISC",
     "private": "true",
     "devDependencies": {
       "@types/eslint": "^8.21.1",
       "@types/jest": "^29.4.0",
       "eslint": "^8.35.0",
       "eslint-config-prettier": "^8.7.0",
       "eslint-plugin-jest": "^27.2.1",
       "jest": "^29.4.3",
       "prettier": "^2.8.4"
     }
   }
```

❶ The --list-different flag tells Prettier to list the names of any files with format-ting issues, rather than emitting their formatted contents. This matches the behavior of ESLint with no flag.

❷ The --loglevel warn flag tells Prettier not to emit any output unless it hits a snag. This matches the behavior of ESLint with no flag.

If you run these scripts, you should see some nice, boring output, since your code is already pretty!

Later on, in Chapter 6, Continuous Integration and Collaboration, on page 123, you'll learn to use these scripts to enforce your code style standards automatically.

That concludes our introduction to Prettier. We've seen how to add Prettier to a project, how to make it play nice with ESLint, and how editor integration makes formatting with Prettier an effortless process.

In the next section you'll meet this chapter's final piece of tooling, an editor extension called Wallaby.

Real-Time Testing with Wallaby

Imagine a world with no boundaries between your code and your tests. Instead of saving changes to your code and seeing the output from Jest in a separate panel, you would see the results of your tests instantly as you type, right before your eyes. Code with passing tests would be marked with a reassuring green. Code with failing tests would be highlighted in red, with a description of the failure floating next to it. Sounds like magic? It's real, and it's called Wallaby.

Note one caveat: Wallaby is a commercial product. We JavaScript developers have been blessed (spoiled, some would say) by an abundance of free tools. All of the other amazing software I've mentioned in this chapter—VS Code, Jest, ESLint, Prettier—is free and open source. The good news is that Wallaby offers a free trial with full functionality, so don't let the price tag deter you from following along with this chapter.

Open up the Extensions sidebar, search for "Wallaby.js", and install. Then open the Command Palette and run Wallaby.js: Select Configuration, then Automatic Configuration <project directory>. Open either palindromes.js or palindromes.test.js and you'll notice new green annotations next to your code, as you can see in the following screenshot.

The annotations are Wallaby's magic sauce. When a line has a green annotation, that means that the line is covered by your tests. If every line in your project's source code has a green annotation, then congrats—you've achieved 100% code coverage!

Try changing the second line of the test to make it fail. Within milliseconds, Wallaby reruns the tests. The failing test line now has a red annotation, meaning that it throws an error (as expect() does when it fails). The specific error is shown next to that line. You can see a full readout by clicking the button in the lower-right corner that shows the number of failing and passing tests in your project or by picking Wallaby.js: Show Failing Tests from the Command Palette. Either way, you should see the output shown in the screenshot on page 41.

Notice that the passing test line has a pink annotation, as does the function body in palindromes.js. The pink annotation means that the line is in the execution path of a failing test. This is an incredibly useful aid for tracking down the cause of test failures since you can rule out all code *not* marked in pink as irrelevant.

Wallaby also has a grey annotation for lines that are not covered by tests and a yellow annotation for lines that are only partly covered by tests.

Seeing your code lit up like a Christmas tree may take some getting used to, but I've come to find Wallaby's annotations invaluable.

A Wallaby Challenge

With Wallaby at the ready, have a go at using TDD to implement the palindrome finder features described by these tests:

```
it("returns an empty array when given no palindromes", () => {
  expect(palindromes("tic tac toe")).toEqual([]);
});

it("ignores casing", () => {
  expect(palindromes("WoW")).toEqual(["wow"]);
});
```

```
it("ignores punctuation", () => {
  expect(palindromes("yo, banana boy!")).toEqual(["yobananaboy"]);
});

it("detects multi-word palindromes", () => {
  expect(palindromes("A man, a plan, a canal, Panama")).toEqual([
    "amanaplanacanalpanama",
  ]);
});
```

This is intended to be a challenge, so don't expect it to be as easy as Fizz Buzz! The important thing is that you learn to take advantage of the real-time feedback provided by Wallaby and the other tools introduced earlier as you work. Be sure to add tests for any utility functions you might write along the way. You can find an example solution at the end of the chapter.

Mantra: Live in the Code

Every time your eyes leave your code, you experience what's known as a context switch. Returning to your code, it's common to feel disoriented, even lost. A TDD workflow that requires you to actively switch between your code and your tests will sap your ability to focus. Hence this chapter's mantra—*Live in the code.* Strive to make running your tests as automatic as breathing.

This chapter introduced you to the VS Code editor, a powerful and endlessly customizable home for your TDD workflow. You learned to use ESLint to preemptively avoid common coding mistakes that tests might miss and to use Prettier to keep your code tidy without losing your momentum. Finally, you tried out Wallaby, which takes TDD to the next level by running your tests continuously as you type and drawing your attention to the code involved with every failure.

In the next chapter, you'll apply these tools to the challenge of writing React components. And you'll add one more important tool to your arsenal—TypeScript.

Example Palindrome Finder Solution

```
ch2/palindromes.test.js
const palindromes = require("./palindromes");
const { prepareStr, isPalindrome, stringStartPalindrome } = palindromes;

describe("prepareStr()", () => {
  it("converts the given string to lowercase", () => {
    expect(prepareStr("aAaA")).toBe("aaaa");
  });

  it("removes all non-letter characters", () => {
    expect(
```

```
      prepareStr("To infinity, and beyond!")
    ).toBe("toinfinityandbeyond");
  });
});

describe("isPalindrome()", () => {
  it("returns true when given a palindrome", () => {
    expect(isPalindrome("aba")).toBe(true);
    expect(isPalindrome("abba")).toBe(true);
  });

  it("returns false when given a non-palindrome", () => {
    expect(isPalindrome("abb")).toBe(false);
    expect(isPalindrome("aaba")).toBe(false);
  });
});

describe("stringStartPalindrome()", () => {
  it("returns the longest palindrome at the start of the string", () => {
    expect(stringStartPalindrome("wow")).toBe("wow");
    expect(stringStartPalindrome("ahha")).toBe("ahha");
    expect(stringStartPalindrome("hohoho")).toBe("hohoh");
  });

  it("returns null if no length 3+ palindrome starts the string", () => {
    expect(stringStartPalindrome("ww")).toBe(null);
    expect(stringStartPalindrome("abcda")).toBe(null);
    expect(stringStartPalindrome("bananarama")).toBe(null);
  });
});

describe("palindromes()", () => {
  it("correctly identifies one-word palindromes", () => {
    expect(palindromes("madam")).toEqual(["madam"]);
    expect(palindromes("racecar")).toEqual(["racecar"]);
  });

  it("returns an empty array when given no palindromes", () => {
    expect(palindromes("tic tac toe")).toEqual([]);
  });

  it("ignores casing", () => {
    expect(palindromes("WoW")).toEqual(["wow"]);
  });

  it("ignores punctuation", () => {
    expect(palindromes("yo, banana boy!")).toEqual(["yobananaboy"]);
  });

  it("detects multi-word palindromes", () => {
    expect(palindromes("A man, a plan, a canal, Panama")).toEqual([
      "amanaplanacanalpanama",
    ]);
  });
});
```

ch2/palindromes.js

```javascript
const prepareStr = str => str.toLowerCase().replace(/[^a-z]/g, '');

const isPalindrome = str => {
  const endIndex = str.length - 1;
  for (let i = 0; i < str.length / 2; i++) {
    if (str[i] !== str[endIndex - i]) return false;
  }
  return true;
};

const stringStartPalindrome = str => {
  const firstLetter = str[0];
  let lastIndex = str.lastIndexOf(firstLetter);
  while (lastIndex >= 2) {
    const candidate = str.substring(0, lastIndex + 1);
    if (isPalindrome(candidate)) {
      return candidate;
    }
    lastIndex = str.lastIndexOf(firstLetter, lastIndex - 1);
  }
  return null;
};

const palindromes = str => {
  const matches = [];
  let startIndex = 0;
  str = prepareStr(str);
  while (startIndex < str.length / 2) {
    const palindrome = stringStartPalindrome(str.substring(startIndex));
    if (palindrome) {
      matches.push(palindrome);
      startIndex += palindrome.length;
    } else {
      startIndex++;
    }
  }
  return matches;
};

// Attach helpers to the exported function for testing
palindromes.prepareStr = prepareStr;
palindromes.isPalindrome = isPalindrome;
palindromes.stringStartPalindrome = stringStartPalindrome;

module.exports = palindromes;
```

CHAPTER 3

Testing React with Testing Library

JavaScript web development can be divided into two eras: pre-React and post-React. Pre-React, all was chaos. Suppose you wanted to make a button toggle a popup when clicked: you'd write HTML for the button, then write an event listener for the button click. The event listener you'd write would directly alter the DOM to show or hide the popup. Code was scattered without rhyme or reason. Unit tests were almost unheard of.

Thankfully, we live in the age of React. Now individual pieces of the app—the button and the popover, in this example—can be isolated as *components*. The DOM tree they render is a pure function of their *props* (React parlance for data provided to the component) and their internal state. And that purity makes them a breeze to test!

In this chapter, you'll use a test-driven approach to build a complex component one piece at a time. You'll learn to use TypeScript along with React's powerful JSX syntax. You'll write unit tests with the simply named Testing Library, a harness that lets you make assertions about the behavior of React components. Along the way, you'll take advantage of the tools introduced in the previous chapter, applying them to a cutting-edge React stack powered by the Vite development server.

Starting a React Project

Our project for this chapter, and for the remainder of the book, will be a carousel component. Carousels have become ubiquitous on the web, yet many implementations fall short in various ways. By building your own, you'll be able to adapt it to your project's needs.

Rather than starting this project from scratch, as in previous chapters, we can take advantage of an existing project template. You'll find an abundance of options for starting a new React project,[1] which fall into two basic categories:

- *Jamstack frameworks* like Next.js, Gatsby, and Remix that are designed for building high-performance production websites. These frameworks add some complexity to enable optimizations like server-side rendering.

- *Static build tools* like Vite and Webpack that compile and bundle JavaScript code but don't provide a server. These simpler tools are great for building React component libraries.

Since we're developing a single React component in this chapter, not an entire website, we'll use Vite. Run this command to set up a new project with Vite that has React and TypeScript built in:

```
$ npm create vite@4.2.0 test-driven-carousel -- --template react-ts

Scaffolding project in ~/code/test-driven-carousel...

Done. Now run:

  cd test-driven-carousel
  npm install
  npm run dev
```

Open the new test-driven-carousel directory in VS Code:

```
$ code test-driven-carousel/
```

Time to start playing around! Run npm install and npm run dev, then open the link shown in your browser. In VS Code, you can open links by holding the primary modifier key (⌘ on macOS, ^ on Windows and Linux) and clicking.

```
$ npm install
$ npm run dev

  VITE v4.4.9  ready in 334 ms

  ➜  Local:   http://localhost:5173/
  ➜  Network: use --host to expose
  ➜  press h to show help
```

---

1. https://react.dev/learn/start-a-new-react-project

You should see a page that looks something like this:

Open up src/App.tsx and edit some of the text (leaving the markup alone for now), then hit save. The page should update with the new text in the blink of an eye, thanks to a technique called hot module reloading (HMR) that allows the Vite dev server to deliver code changes to the browser without a full refresh. As shown in the screenshot on page 48.

Time to save your progress. Use VS Code's Git: Initialize Repository command, or run the following command:

```
$ git init
```

Once the repo is initialized, add the .gitignore from the previous chapter:

```
ch3/.gitignore
node_modules/
.vscode/
```

Then make an initial commit:

```
:tada: First commit
```

So far, so familiar. But what is this tsx syntax, exactly?

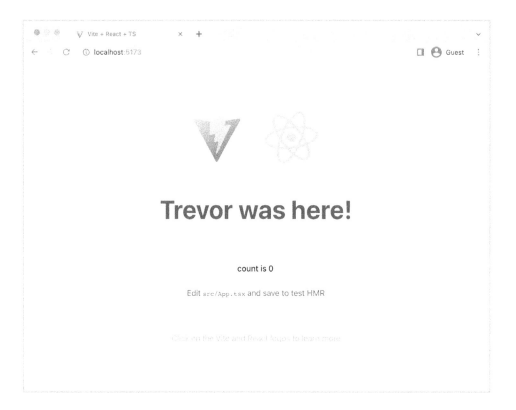

Combining Markup with Code using JSX and TSX

Like any other JavaScript library, React is fully usable through plain, ordinary JavaScript code. But hardly anyone uses it that way. Instead, they compile a language called JSX down to ordinary JavaScript.

JSX allows HTML-like markup to be embedded within JavaScript code. When the code is compiled to pure JavaScript that a web browser can understand, each JSX tag is converted to a function call that tells React what kind of element to create. So for instance, take a look at the following code:

```
const helloJSX = <h1 className="super-big">Hello, JSX!</h1>;
```

It would compile to something like this:

```
const helloJSX = React.createElement(
  'h1',
  { className: 'super-big' },
  'Hello, JSX!'
);
```

If you're new to JSX, this new syntax will take some getting used to. But it makes code much easier to read and write than the equivalent series of React.createElement() calls would be. For more details on JSX syntax, take a look at the React docs.[2]

Our project uses TSX, which is a combination of TypeScript and JSX. For the most part, TypeScript code looks identical to JavaScript code apart from having type annotations. You'll learn more about TypeScript later in this chapter. In the meantime, if you want to experiment with TSX yourself, check out the TypeScript playground.[3] You can enter TSX code there and see the compiled JS output in real time!

An Ode to CoffeeScript

My first book was on CoffeeScript, a language introduced by Jeremy Ashkenas in 2009 as "a little language that compiles into JavaScript." CoffeeScript was hugely influential in two respects: first, it pioneered a number of syntax features that would make their way into the ECMAScript 6 standard, and second, it was the first compile-to-JavaScript language to catch on, paving the way for the success of JSX and TypeScript.

CoffeeScript's time has passed, but today's JavaScripters may have it to thank for kicking off an era of innovation for the once stagnant language. I'm proud to have played a small role in bringing it to the world's attention.

Our Vite project is already set up to compile TSX code for you automatically. Just be aware that what's sent to the browser is plain, ordinary JavaScript. Browsers can't run JSX or TypeScript directly.

Right now you may feel as though you're walking across a tightrope without a net. Not to worry—in the next section, we'll add ESLint and Prettier to the project, including a bevy of TypeScript-specific linter rules that will help keep your code on track.

Setting up ESLint and Prettier for React and TypeScript

A remarkable virtue of ESLint is that it can lint more than just vanilla Java-Script. Thanks to its pluggable architecture, it can also lint languages that transpile to JavaScript, including TSX. In this section, we'll extend the configuration from the previous chapter to do just that.

---

2. https://react.dev/learn/writing-markup-with-jsx
3. https://www.typescriptlang.org/play?#code/JYWwDg9gTgLgBAJQKYEMDG8BmUljgcilQ3wG4BYAKCrQgDsBneA-CyQBs2lApAZQA04AXjgAeZgGY4NigYMAcihBJBAlgYBXMEigBaAEbAA5qoB8ACXacANHF58AhCID0E0xWqUgA

Start by installing the ESLint and Prettier dependencies from the last chapter, with the exception of eslint-plugin-jest, which we won't be needing:

```
$ npm install --save-dev eslint@8.35.0 @types/eslint@8.21.1 \
  prettier@2.8.4 eslint-config-prettier@8.7.0
```

The initial configuration files will look just like those in the last chapter but with one change: instead of the .js extension, use .cjs. The .cjs extension indicates these files are CommonJS, the default module format in Node. Vite prefers ESM, which the JavaScript ecosystem is gradually moving toward, so our project has the declaration "type": "module" in its package.json, which makes Node treat .js files as ESM instead of CommonJS. For the most part you won't have to worry about Common-JS vs. ESM in this book. One nice thing about TypeScript is that it's always written in ESM format, so the details of module resolution are left to the build tools.

With that in mind, add these ESLint and Prettier configuration files to the project:

```
// .eslintrc.cjs
/** @type {import('eslint').Linter.Config} */
module.exports = {
  extends: ["eslint:recommended", "prettier"],
  env: {
    node: true,
    es2021: true,
  },
  overrides: [{ files: ["*.cjs"] }],
};
```

❶ By default, ESLint only lints files with the .js extension. To make it cover .cjs files, there are two options: either specify --ext .cjs every time we call the ESLint command, or add an overrides entry to the config for *.cjs files. The overrides entry may look a little strange since it isn't actually overriding anything, but it's less effort than the alternative.

```
// .prettierrc.cjs
module.exports = {};
```

Copy the lint and format scripts from the last chapter into package.json:

```
// package.json
  ...
  "scripts": {
    "dev": "vite",
    "lint": "eslint . && prettier --list-different .",
    "format": "eslint --fix . && prettier --loglevel warn --write .",
    "build": "tsc && vite build",
    "preview": "vite preview"
  },
  ...
```

Finally, now that we have a build step, we'll want to make sure that ESLint and Prettier ignore our build output. To do that, create two new files called .eslintignore and .prettierignore:

```
# .eslintignore
dist
```

```
# .prettierignore
dist
```

Now you can run the lint command, which should report 0 issues. If you run the format command, you'll see some slight changes to the .ts and .tsx files that came with the project. That's because Prettier covers TypeScript/TSX right out of the box. ESLint will need a little help, though, in the form of a project called typescript-eslint.[4]

The typescript-eslint project consists of two packages, a parser and a plugin. Install both:

```
$ npm install --save-dev @typescript-eslint/parser \
  @typescript-eslint/eslint-plugin
```

Now add an overrides entry to the ESLint configuration for TypeScript files:

```
// .eslintrc.cjs
/** @type {import('eslint').Linter.Config} */
module.exports = {
  extends: ["eslint:recommended", "prettier"],
  env: {
    node: true,
    es2021: true,
  },
  overrides: [
    { files: ["*.cjs"] },
    {
      files: ["*.ts", "*.tsx"],
      extends: [
        "plugin:@typescript-eslint/recommended",
        "plugin:@typescript-eslint/recommended-requiring-type-checking",
      ],
      plugins: ["@typescript-eslint"],
      parser: "@typescript-eslint/parser",
      parserOptions: {
        project: true,
        tsconfigRootDir: __dirname,
      },
    },
  ],
};
```

---

4. https://typescript-eslint.io/

❶ The plugin:@typescript-eslint/recommended config is pretty minimalist. It exists mainly to disable rules from the eslint:recommended config that are redundant with TypeScript.

❷ The plugin:@typescript-eslint/recommended-requiring-type-checking config is more interesting. To quote the typescript-eslint docs, this config enables rules that "utilize the awesome power of TypeScript's typechecking APIs to provide much deeper insights into your code." One useful rule in this set is the no-floating-promises rule, which requires you to handle promises returned by async functions you call (for example, by using the await keyword). Treating async functions as if they were synchronous is a common developer mistake, but thanks to the combined power of Type-Script and ESLint, you don't have to worry about it!

If you run the npm lint run command now, ESLint will report any issues it sees in the project's TypeScript (and TSX) files.

One more addition to ESLint is in order: since we'll be working with React in this project, we'll benefit from adding React-specific rules. To do that, install the eslint-plugin-react package:

```
$ npm install --save-dev eslint-plugin-react@7.32.2
```

Then add two entries to the extends field in .eslintrc.cjs to bring in rules from the plugin, and a new settings block that tells the plugin to detect the React version that's installed:

```
// .eslintrc.cjs
/** @type {import('eslint').Linter.Config} */
module.exports = {
  extends: [
    "eslint:recommended",
    "prettier",
➤    "plugin:react/recommended",
➤    "plugin:react/jsx-runtime",
  ],
➤  settings: {
➤    react: {
➤      version: "detect",
➤    },
➤  },
  env: {
    node: true,
    es2021: true,
  },
  overrides: [
    { files: ["*.cjs"] },
    {
```

```
      files: ["*.ts", "*.tsx"],
      extends: [
        "plugin:@typescript-eslint/recommended",
        "plugin:@typescript-eslint/recommended-requiring-type-checking",
      ],
      plugins: ["@typescript-eslint"],
      parser: "@typescript-eslint/parser",
      parserOptions: {
        project: true,
        tsconfigRootDir: __dirname,
      },
    },
  ],
};
```

If you run the lint script now, you'll see that one of the new rules is failing:

```
$ npm run lint
/Users/tburnham/code/test-driven-carousel/src/App.tsx
  12:9  error  Using target="_blank" without rel="noreferrer"
  (which implies rel="noopener") is a security risk in older browsers:
  see https://mathiasbynens.github.io/rel-noopener/#recommendations
    react/jsx-no-target-blank
```

This is a helpful rule! But we're not going to need the contents of App.tsx, so we might as well get rid of that code. You can replace App.tsx with this place-holder for now:

```
export default function App() {
  return null;
}
```

Commit your work so far:

```
:wrench: Set up ESLint and Prettier
```

In the next section, we'll incorporate unit tests into our project using Vite's test runner, Vitest.

Adding Unit Tests with Vitest

In the previous chapters, you used Jest as your test runner. But for Vite projects, the preferred test runner is Vitest. Thankfully, Vitest was designed as a drop-in replacement for Jest. So once Vitest is set up, the experience of writing tests for it should feel familiar.

To start, install the vitest package:

```
$ npm install --save-dev vitest@0.34.1
```

Next, update the scripts entry in package.json to make Vitest the project's official test runner:

```
// package.json
{
  ...
  "scripts": {
    "dev": "vite",
    "lint": "eslint . && prettier --list-different .",
    "format": "eslint --fix . && prettier --loglevel warn --write .",
    "test": "vitest",
    "build": "tsc && vite build",
    "preview": "vite preview"
  },
  ...
}
```

By default, Vitest requires you to import basic functions like describe and expect. To make these available as globals, you'll need to make a couple of configuration tweaks. First, update vite.config.tsx to use the defineConfig function from vitest/config, and enable the test.globals flag:

```
// vite.config.ts
import { defineConfig } from "vitest/config";
import react from "@vitejs/plugin-react";

// https://vitejs.dev/config/
export default defineConfig({
  plugins: [react()],
  test: {
    globals: true,
  },
});
```

Then add a types entry to tsconfig.json so that TypeScript will recognize the new globals:

```
ch3/tsconfig.json
{
  "compilerOptions": {
    "target": "ESNext",
    "useDefineForClassFields": true,
    "lib": ["DOM", "DOM.Iterable", "ESNext"],
    "types": ["vitest/globals"],
    "allowJs": false,
    "skipLibCheck": true,
    "esModuleInterop": false,
    "allowSyntheticDefaultImports": true,
    "strict": true,
    "forceConsistentCasingInFileNames": true,
    "module": "ESNext",
```

```
    "moduleResolution": "Node",
    "resolveJsonModule": true,
    "isolatedModules": true,
    "noEmit": true,
    "jsx": "react-jsx"
  },
  "include": ["src", "vite.config.ts"],
  "references": [{ "path": "./tsconfig.node.json" }]
}
```

Now you're ready to create a test:

```
// src/example.test.ts
describe('Example test', () => {
  it('works', () => {
    expect(1).toBe(1);
  })
})
```

Try running the test script, which will start Vitest in watch mode:

```
$ npm run test

 ✓ src/example.test.ts (1)

 Test Files  1 passed (1)
      Tests  1 passed (1)
   Start at  18:11:14
   Duration  166ms


 PASS  Waiting for file changes...
       press h to show help, press q to quit
```

Notice how quickly that test ran! Vite is famous for its efficient build pipeline, which Vitest integrates into neatly.

Commit the configuration change:

```
:wrench: Set up Vitest
```

Next, we'll add one last supporting technology before we switch into TDD mode—Wallaby.

Running Wallaby

If you're using VS Code with the Wallaby.tsx extension, as described in the previous chapter, (#sec.testing-with-wallaby), then starting Wallaby in this project is a simple two-step process:

1. Open the Command Palette and select Wallaby.tsx: Select Configuration, then Automatic Configuration <project directory>. You'll only need to do this once for each project you use Wallaby in.

2. Open the Command Palette again and select Wallaby.tsx: Start.

Open up example.test.ts and you should see the familiar green annotations showing that the test is passing.

Now you're ready to build your first test-driven React component!

Testing Simple Components with React Testing Library

It's time to start building the carousel component that will be your project for the rest of this book. A carousel is a widget that shows a series of images to the user one at a time. The user has the ability to move between adjacent images in the series. The carousel can also auto-advance, like a slideshow. By the end of the book, our carousel will look like this:

Seattle Photo by Ganapathy Kumar on Unsplash

Prev   Next

Since this is fairly complex, we're going to implement it as a primary component called Carousel with two secondary components:

1. CarouselSlide, an image shown in the carousel
2. CarouselButton, a button that lets the user control the slides

Let's start by writing some tests for the simplest component. CarouselButton is just going to render a <button>. (Why componentize it at all? Because we're going to add styling to that <button> in the next chapter.) We'll make assertions about the component using a library called React Testing Library (RTL).

Enzyme vs. React Testing Library

When I was writing the first edition of this book back in 2019, React Testing Library was still in its infancy. The most popular library for testing React components was called Enzyme. The two libraries had competing philosophies; Enzyme was oriented toward making assertions about the components themselves, including their internal state, while React Testing Library was oriented toward making assertions about the *output* of components, namely the DOM they render.

Both testing philosophies have their advantages in different scenarios, but what ultimately did Enzyme in wasn't its philosophy, it was React itself. When React moved from classes to hooks, many of Enzyme's APIs simply stopped working. For one thing, React doesn't provide a mechanism for inspecting state in hooks, making testing internal state impossible.

These days, React Testing Library is by far the most popular way to test React components, and I've grown to embrace its DOM-oriented testing philosophy.

Getting Started with React Testing Library

It's time to install React Testing Library, along with some dependencies:

```
$ npm install --save-dev @testing-library/react@14.0.0 happy-dom@9.20.3 \
    @testing-library/jest-dom@6.0.0
```

The first dependency is React Testing Library itself. The other two dependencies relate to the DOM, the object hierarchy used by web browsers to keep track of all the elements on the page:

- The happy-dom[5] library is a JavaScript implementation of the DOM. React expects to interact with the DOM, so a simulated DOM is a prerequisite for running React code. As of this writing, the most popular simulated DOM is JSDOM; happy-dom is a newer, more performant alternative that's well supported by Vitest.

- The jest-dom[6] extension for testing-library allows you to make assertions about the state of the DOM in our tests, as you'll soon see.

Integrating all of these packages into Vitest requires some small configuration changes:

ch3/vite.config.ts
```
import { defineConfig } from "vitest/config";
import react from "@vitejs/plugin-react";

// https://vitejs.dev/config/
```

---

5.   https://github.com/capricorn86/happy-dom
6.   https://github.com/testing-library/jest-dom

```
export default defineConfig({
  plugins: [react()],
  test: {
    globals: true,
    environment: "happy-dom",
    setupFiles: ["test-setup.ts"],
  },
});
```

The test-setup.ts file referenced from the config will install the matchers for DOM assertions, saving you the trouble of having to import them in every test:

ch3/test-setup.ts
```
import "@testing-library/jest-dom/vitest";
```

One more bit of setup—an official ESLint plugin for React Testing Library has rules designed to guard against common mistakes. Go ahead and install it:

```
$ npm install --save-dev eslint-plugin-testing-library@6.0.1
```

Then add plugin:testing-library/react to the extends list in your ESLint config to enable the recommended rules:

ch3/.eslintrc.cjs
```
/** @type {import('eslint').Linter.Config} */
module.exports = {
  extends: [
    "eslint:recommended",
    "prettier",
    "plugin:react/recommended",
    "plugin:react/jsx-runtime",
    "plugin:testing-library/react",
  ],
  settings: {
    react: {
      version: "detect",
    },
  },
  env: {
    node: true,
    es2021: true,
  },
  overrides: [
    { files: ["*.cjs"] },
    {
      files: ["*.ts", "*.tsx"],
      extends: [
        "plugin:@typescript-eslint/recommended",
        "plugin:@typescript-eslint/recommended-requiring-type-checking",
      ],
      plugins: ["@typescript-eslint"],
```

```
      parser: "@typescript-eslint/parser",
      parserOptions: {
        project: true,
        tsconfigRootDir: __dirname,
      },
    },
  ],
};
```

Now you're ready to write some component tests! You can delete the example.test.ts file. Then define a minimal implementation of CarouselButton so you have something to run tests against:

```
// src/CarouselButton.tsx
const CarouselButton = () => <button />;

export default CarouselButton;
```

CarouselButton is defined as a function that returns an empty <button>. Simple as it is, this is a valid React component, which is all we need to run tests against it. Our plan is to add test cases (which will fail at first) and then modify the component as needed to make them pass.

Now put this test in place:

```
import { render, screen } from "@testing-library/react";
import CarouselButton from "./CarouselButton";

describe("CarouselButton", () => {
  it("renders a <button>", () => {
❶   render(<CarouselButton />);
❷   expect(screen.getByRole("button")).toBeInTheDocument();
  });
});
```

❶ The render function does what it says on the tin—it takes a React element and renders it to the DOM. Note the simulated DOM is automatically reset for every test.

❷ The screen.getByRole function is built in to Testing Library. It finds a single element in the DOM with the given ARIA role; it'll throw an error if no elements match or if more than one element matches. The toBeInTheDocument matcher comes from @testing-library/jest-dom. Given the behavior of getByRole, the matcher is redundant, but it makes the test more readable.

If you run npm test, the test output should be all-green. However, savvy React developers will notice that this isn't a very useful CarouselButton implementation yet—there's no way to put content inside of the <button />. So let's get into full TDD mode, after we commit using the gitmoji for a work in progress:

```
:construction: Starting work on CarouselButton
```

Working with Props

Currently, CarouselButton renders an empty <button> element, which isn't very useful. We need to add support for setting the children of the <button> element, which will be the text that the user sees. Add a test for that to the existing describe() block:

```
// src/CarouselButton.test.tsx
...
it("passes `children` through to the <button>", () => {
  const text = "Button text";
  render(<CarouselButton>{text}</CarouselButton>);
  expect(screen.getByRole("button")).toHaveTextContent("Button text");
});
...
```

Currently that button is rendered without children, failing the test. Your editor may also indicate a TypeScript error, as CarouselButton doesn't currently take any props. To fix that, add some prop-passing logic to the component:

```
// src/CarouselButton.tsx
const CarouselButton = ({ children }) => <button>{children}</button>;
...
```

When a component is defined as a function, that function receives the component instance's props object as the first argument. The argument list ({ children }) uses the object destructuring syntax to extract props.children as children, which is then passed through to the rendered <button>.

By the way, in JSX syntax the children prop is special. We have two different ways to pass the prop in. For example, the two lines of code that follow are equivalent:

```
<button>{children}</button>
```

```
<button children={children} />
```

Anything inserted between an opening tag and a closing tag is treated as that element's children prop. (If children is set in both places, the value between the tags has precedence.)

With that component change, your tests should be in the green! However, you may notice that the typechecker is still unhappy, as is the linter. If you run npm run lint, you'll see this error:

```
'children' is missing in props validation (react/prop-types)
```

Since you're using the recommended ESLint config from the React plugin, you're going to see a lot of constructive criticism like this. In this case, it wants you to declare a type for the children prop. Back in the early days of React, the standard way to do that was to attach a propTypes object to the component to validate the types at runtime and emit a console warning. Happily, we can do better now—if we declare the type with TypeScript, the checker will guarantee that all props that are passed in at runtime conform to that type!

TypeScript types are declared with the syntax <variable>: <type>. Combined with the object destructuring syntax, that looks like this:

```
// src/CarouselButton.tsx
import React from 'react';
import { ReactNode } from "react";

const CarouselButton = ({ children }: { children?: ReactNode }) => (
  <button>{children}</button>
);

export default CarouselButton;
```

Here the variable we're declaring a type for is the props argument. The type declaration { children?: ReactNode } says that the children prop, if given (the ?: syntax means it's optional), must be a ReactNode. The ReactNode type means that anything React can render (including React elements and strings) is allowed.

Run npm run lint again to confirm that we're now in the clear. You can also run the typechecker with npx tsc --noEmit. In both cases, no output means that we have a clean bill of health!

Now that the linter and typechecker are satisfied, let's think ahead to what other functionality CarouselButton needs to support. In addition to passing children through to the button, we'll want to support passing an onClick event handler through. We'll also want to support passing a className prop through for styling. And we'll want to support data- attributes too. Come to think of it, what if we just pass *every* prop supported by the <button> element through by default?

This is actually a very common practice in React, and a sensible one. Add another test to the existing describe() block with more prop assertions:

```
// src/CarouselButton.test.tsx
...
it("passes other props through to the <button>", () => {
  const className = "my-carousel-button";
  const dataAction = "prev";
  render(
    <CarouselButton className={className} data-action={dataAction}>
      Button text
    </CarouselButton>
  );
  expect(screen.getByRole("button")).toHaveClass(className);
```

```
➤    expect(screen.getByRole("button")).toHaveAttribute(
➤      "data-action",
➤      dataAction
➤    );
➤  });
   ...
```

❶ Typically, React props use camelCase, like className. But data- props are
always hyphenated (as are aria- props, which we'll meet later). Data props
have no meaning in the DOM; they're a way of attaching arbitrary key-
value pairs to elements.

To satisfy the new test, update CarouselButton to pass all props through:

ch3/src/CarouselButton.tsx
```
import { ComponentPropsWithRef } from "react";

const CarouselButton = (props: ComponentPropsWithRef<"button">) => (
  <button {...props} />
);

export default CarouselButton;
```

❶ {...props} is the JSX spread operator. It's equivalent to passing each prop
in the props object through individually. That includes children, since the
tag itself has no children.

And we're back in the green! This is a good point for a commit:

```
:sparkles: Initial implementation of CarouselButton
```

Now it's time to build CarouselButton's sibling, CarouselSlide.

Testing Nested Markup

So far, we've used React to encapsulate the functionality of a single DOM
element (<button>) in a component (CarouselButton). But React components are
capable of doing more than that.

We're going to build a component called CarouselSlide, which will be responsible
for rendering several distinct DOM elements:

- An <img> to display the actual image
- A <figcaption> to associate caption text with the image
- Text, some of which will be wrapped in <strong> for emphasis
- A <figure> to wrap it all up

We'll take a TDD approach to building this tree while ensuring that the props
we provide to CarouselSlide are routed correctly. Start by creating a *stub* of the
component, a minimal implementation you can add functionality to later:

```
// src/CarouselSlide.tsx
const CarouselSlide = () => <figure />;

export default CarouselSlide;
```

Now for the tests! A good way to start is to check that the right type of DOM element is rendered:

```
// src/CarouselSlide.test.tsx
import { render, screen } from "@testing-library/react";
import CarouselSlide from "./CarouselSlide";

describe("CarouselSlide", () => {
  it("renders a <figure>", () => {
    render(<CarouselSlide />);
    expect(screen.getByRole("figure")).toBeInTheDocument();
  });
});
```

This test should be green. So let's add more requirements. We want the <figure> to contain two children: an <img> and a <figcaption>. To express that in a test, you'll need to write Testing Library queries for those elements. Testing Library encourages the use of ARIA roles when possible; that way, tests are aligned with best practices for writing accessible markup. The <img> tag has an associated ARIA role—"img". The <figcaption> tag, on the other hand, does not. So we'll use the data-testid attribute again to make it easy to select:

```
// src/CarouselSlide.test.tsx
//...
➤ it("renders an <img> and a <figcaption>", () => {
➤   render(<CarouselSlide />);
➤   const figure = screen.getByRole("figure");
➤   const img = screen.getByRole("img");
➤   const figcaption = screen.getByTestId("caption");
➤   expect(figure).toContainElement(img);
➤   expect(figure).toContainElement(figcaption);
➤ });
  //...
```

The new test will be red since <img> and <figcaption> don't yet exist. Add them to the CarouselSlide render tree:

```
// src/CarouselSlide.tsx
➤ const CarouselSlide = () => (
➤   <figure>
➤     <img />
➤     <figcaption data-testid="caption" />
➤   </figure>
➤ );

export default CarouselSlide;
```

That should put you in the green. Next, we need to add content. For that, we'll supply three props:

1. imgUrl, a URL for the image displayed in the slide
2. description, a short piece of caption text
3. attribution, the name of the image's author

The imgUrl will be used as the src for the <img> tag. Add a test:

```
// src/CarouselSlide.test.tsx
...
it("passes `imgUrl` through to the <img>", () => {
  const imgUrl = "https://example.com/image.png";
  render(<CarouselSlide imgUrl={imgUrl} />);
  expect(screen.getByRole("img")).toHaveAttribute("src", imgUrl);
});
...
```

Modify CarouselSlide so that the imgUrl test turns green:

```
// src/CarouselSlide.tsx
const CarouselSlide = ({ imgUrl }: { imgUrl?: string }) => (
  <figure>
    <img src={imgUrl} />
    <figcaption data-testid="caption" />
  </figure>
);

export default CarouselSlide;
```

Now let's add another requirement. We want to add props called description and attribution, and we want both to be rendered in <figcaption>, with the description bolded by a <strong> tag:

```
// src/CarouselSlide.test.tsx
...
it("uses `description` and `attribution` as the caption", () => {
  const props = {
    description: "A jaw-droppingly spectacular image",
    attribution: "Trevor Burnham",
  };
  render(<CarouselSlide {...props} />);
  const figcaption = screen.getByTestId("caption");
  expect(figcaption).toHaveTextContent(
    `${props.description} ${props.attribution}`
  );
});
...
```

Try making all tests pass. When you're done, your implementation should look something like this:

```
// src/CarouselSlide.tsx
import { ReactNode } from "react";

const CarouselSlide = ({
  imgUrl,
  description,
  attribution,
}: {
  imgUrl?: string;
  description?: ReactNode;
  attribution?: ReactNode;
}) => (
  <figure>
    <img src={imgUrl} />
    <figcaption data-testid="caption">
      <strong>{description}</strong> {attribution}
    </figcaption>
  </figure>
);

export default CarouselSlide;
```

One feature is still missing from the component: to support styling, we should pass the className and style props through to the <figure>. In fact, for maximum flexibility, we should allow event handlers, data- attributes, and so on. In short, we should pass every prop *except* the three we're explicitly using through to the <figure>.

Add a test that sets an arbitrary assortment of props as the finishing touch on CarouselSlide.test.tsx for this chapter:

```
ch3/src/CarouselSlide.test.tsx
import { render, screen } from "@testing-library/react";
import CarouselSlide from "./CarouselSlide";

describe("CarouselSlide", () => {
  it("renders a <figure>", () => {
    render(<CarouselSlide />);
    expect(screen.getByRole("figure")).toBeInTheDocument();
  });

  it("renders an <img> and a <figcaption>", () => {
    render(<CarouselSlide />);
    const figure = screen.getByRole("figure");
    const img = screen.getByRole("img");
    const figcaption = screen.getByTestId("caption");
    expect(figure).toContainElement(img);
    expect(figure).toContainElement(figcaption);
  });

  it("passes `imgUrl` through to the <img>", () => {
    const imgUrl = "https://example.com/image.png";
```

```
    render(<CarouselSlide imgUrl={imgUrl} />);
    expect(screen.getByRole("img")).toHaveAttribute("src", imgUrl);
  });

  it("uses `description` and `attribution` as the caption", () => {
    const props = {
      description: "A jaw-droppingly spectacular image",
      attribution: "Trevor Burnham",
    };
    render(<CarouselSlide {...props} />);
    const figcaption = screen.getByTestId("caption");
    expect(figcaption).toHaveTextContent(
      `${props.description} ${props.attribution}`
    );
  });

  it("passes other props through to the <figure>", () => {
    const props = {
      className: "my-carousel-slide",
      "data-test-name": "My slide",
    };
    render(<CarouselSlide {...props} />);
    const figure = screen.getByRole("figure");
    expect(figure).toHaveClass(props.className);
    expect(figure).toHaveAttribute("data-test-name", props["data-test-name"]);
  });
});
```

The most common way to implement this functionality is with the *object rest syntax.* Here's what it looks like:

```
ch3/src/CarouselSlide.tsx
import { ComponentPropsWithRef, ReactNode } from "react";

const CarouselSlide = ({
  imgUrl,
  description,
  attribution,
  ...rest
}: {
  imgUrl?: string;
  description?: ReactNode;
  attribution?: ReactNode;
} & ComponentPropsWithRef<"figure">) => (
  <figure {...rest}>
    <img src={imgUrl} />
    <figcaption data-testid="caption">
      <strong>{description}</strong> {attribution}
    </figcaption>
  </figure>
);

export default CarouselSlide;
```

As before, the function only takes a single argument that's destructured into individual variables. However, now there's an object named rest that collects all values from the props object that haven't been explicitly destructured.

Conversely, the JSX spread {...rest} takes the key-value pairs from the rest object and converts them into props. Since rest was originally created from the leftover props given to CarouselSlide, the effect is to pass those props—everything but imgUrl, description, and attribution—through to the <figure>.

You may be familiar with the rest/spread syntax from argument lists and arrays, where it's been supported since ES6. The object rest/spread syntax is newer and was added to the language as part of the ES2018 specification.

CarouselSlide and its tests should be looking shipshape now! Make a commit:

```
:sparkles: Initial implementation of CarouselSlide
```

Just one component to go—Carousel itself.

Testing Stateful Components

Both of the React components we've built so far are *stateless*; their render output is determined entirely by the props they receive, allowing us to express them as a single function. This has the advantage of simplicity. But a carousel is *stateful*; it needs to keep track of which slide it's currently showing. In this section, we'll take a TDD approach to building a Carousel component with internal state.

Writing Components with TDD

Start with a stub implementation of the component:

```
// src/Carousel.tsx
const Carousel = () => {
  return <div data-testid="carousel" />;
};

export default Carousel;
```

The data-testid attribute is a common convention in React Testing Library to make a specific element easily selectable in a test. To use it, pass the attribute value into the getByTestId() selector:

```
// src/Carousel.test.tsx
import { render, screen } from "@testing-library/react";
import Carousel from "./Carousel";
```

```
describe("Carousel", () => {
  it("renders a <div>", () => {
    render(<Carousel />);
    expect(screen.getByTestId("carousel")).toBeInTheDocument();
  });
});
```

That test should be in the green. Now to start iterating!

When writing a component, it's usually a good idea to start with the core functionality. In this case, the core functionality of the carousel is to accept a list of slides and display one of them. We'll ignore slide-changing controls for now and just display the first slide.

Add a test:

```
// src/Carousel.test.tsx
...
describe("Carousel", () => {
  const slides = [
    {
      imgUrl: 'https://example.com/slide1.png',
      description: 'Slide 1',
      attribution: 'Uno Pizzeria',
    },
    {
      imgUrl: 'https://example.com/slide2.png',
      description: 'Slide 2',
      attribution: 'Dos Equis',
    },
    {
      imgUrl: 'https://example.com/slide3.png',
      description: 'Slide 3',
      attribution: 'Three Amigos',
    },
  ];
  ...
  it("renders the first slide by default", () => {
    render(<Carousel slides={slides} />);
    const img = screen.getByRole("img");
    expect(img).toHaveAttribute("src", slides[0].imgUrl);
  });
})
```

To satisfy the new test, update Carousel to accept an array of objects with the properties of each slide and pass the first slide object down to CarouselSlide:

```
// src/Carousel.tsx
import { ReactNode } from "react";
import CarouselSlide from "./CarouselSlide";
```

```
① type Slide = {
     imgUrl?: string;
     description?: ReactNode;
     attribution?: ReactNode;
   };
② const Carousel = ({slides}: {slides?: Slide[]}) => {
     return (
       <div data-testid="carousel">
③        <CarouselSlide {...slides?.[0]} />
       </div>
     );
   };

   export default Carousel;
```

❶ This is the first time we've declared a type separately from an argument list, using the type keyword. That allows us to reference the type by name. Later on, we might want to refactor Carousel and CarouselSlide to both consume this type rather than duplicate the imgUrl, description, and attribution declarations.

❷ The Slide[] syntax indicates an array of items that match the Slide type. TypeScript also supports the equivalent syntax Array<Slide>.

❸ Remember the prop spread operator? We used the syntax {...rest} to pass each key-value pair from the rest object as a separate prop. Here we're doing the same, but with the slides[0] object, and only if it exists: the syntax slides?.[0] returns undefined if slides itself is undefined, and spreading undefined has no effect.

The tests should be in the green again, which means that the first slide is successfully rendering. Commit your work so far:

```
:sparkles: Initial implementation of Carousel
```

Now let's outline some requirements for making this component a true carousel:

- The carousel keeps track of the current slide with a number, slideIndex.

- slideIndex is initially 0, meaning that the first slide is shown.

- Clicking the Prev button decreases slideIndex, wrapping around to the index of the last slide when it would go below 0.

- Clicking the Next button increases slideIndex, wrapping around to 0 when it would go above the index of the last slide.

- The carousel takes an array named slides and renders the slide indicated by slideIndex.

Translating these requirements into tests will help us figure out exactly how to implement them.

Testing Interactions

Unlike Enzyme, React Testing Library (RTL) doesn't allow internal state to be accessed directly. The inner workings of the component are treated as a black box. So here's what our standard approach to testing a component's state will be:

1. Render the component.
2. Simulate a user interaction.
3. Check that the component's DOM output changes as we'd expect.

To simulate user interactions, we'll need an additional dependency:

```
$ npm install --save-dev @testing-library/user-event@14.4.3
```

That addition yields the final package.json for the chapter:

ch3/package.json
```
{
  "name": "test-driven-carousel",
  "private": true,
  "version": "0.0.0",
  "type": "module",
  "scripts": {
    "dev": "vite",
    "lint": "eslint . && prettier --list-different .",
    "format": "eslint --fix . && prettier --log-level warn --write .",
    "build": "tsc && vite build",
    "test": "vitest",
    "preview": "vite preview"
  },
  "dependencies": {
    "react": "^18.2.0",
    "react-dom": "^18.2.0"
  },
  "devDependencies": {
    "@testing-library/jest-dom": "^6.0.0",
    "@testing-library/react": "^14.0.0",
    "@testing-library/user-event": "^14.4.3",
    "@types/eslint": "^8.21.1",
    "@types/react": "^18.0.28",
    "@types/react-dom": "^18.0.11",
    "@typescript-eslint/eslint-plugin": "^5.58.0",
    "@typescript-eslint/parser": "^5.58.0",
    "@vitejs/plugin-react": "^4.0.4",
    "eslint": "^8.35.0",
    "eslint-config-prettier": "^8.7.0",
    "eslint-plugin-react": "^7.32.2",
    "happy-dom": "^9.20.3",
    "prettier": "^2.8.4",
```

```
    "typescript": "^4.9.3",
    "vite": "^4.4.9",
    "vitest": "^0.34.1"
  }
}
```

The carousel requirements from the previous section imply two possible interactions—clicking the Prev button and clicking the Next button. Start by adding a test for the Next button:

```
// src/Carousel.test.tsx
import { render, screen } from "@testing-library/react";
import userEvent from "@testing-library/user-event";
import Carousel from "./Carousel";
...
it("advances the slide when the Next button is clicked", async () => {
  render(<Carousel slides={slides} />);
  const img = screen.getByRole("img");
  const nextButton = screen.getByTestId("next-button");
  const user = userEvent.setup();

  await user.click(nextButton);
  expect(img).toHaveAttribute("src", slides[1].imgUrl);
  await user.click(nextButton);
  expect(img).toHaveAttribute("src", slides[2].imgUrl);
  await user.click(nextButton);
  expect(img).toHaveAttribute("src", slides[0].imgUrl);
});
...
```

❶ Notice that this test is declared as an async function so that it can use the await keyword to perform asynchronous actions.

❷ Simulated user events in Testing Library are always async functions. That allows the event to fully resolve, and the DOM to update, before the test continues. A common mistake developers make is failing to await an async function call; fortunately, the no-floating-promises rule in typescript-eslint (enabled as part of @typescript-eslint/recommended-requiring-type-checking) will catch this!

To satisfy this test, Carousel needs state to track the slide index and a button that increments that slide index (wrapping it around to 0 if it would overflow the list of slides):

```
// src/Carousel.tsx
...
const Carousel = ({ slides }: { slides?: Slide[] }) => {
  const [slideIndex, setSlideIndex] = useState(0);
  return (
    <div data-testid="carousel">
      <CarouselSlide {...slides?.[slideIndex]} />
```

```
      <CarouselButton
        data-testid="next-button"
        onClick={() => {
          if (!slides) return;
          setSlideIndex((i) => (i + 1) % slides.length);
        }}
      >
        Next
      </CarouselButton>
    </div>
  );
};
...
```

❶ The syntax useState(0) means "Use 0 as the initial value of this state."

❷ State setters like setSlideIndex can accept either a raw value or a callback function. The callback takes the existing state value as an argument and returns the new value. We're using the callback rather than setSlideIndex((slideIndex + 1) % slides.length) to handle a rare edge case: it's possible for the user to click the button twice before Carousel re-renders, in which case the onClick handler for the second click would see the same slideIndex value as the first click, making the direct setter a no-op.

The % sign on this line is the remainder operator, which handles the overflow case.

That should satisfy the Next test. Now repeat the test-and-implement process for the Prev button. (One gotcha to keep in mind—the remainder operator doesn't work for negative numbers!) Your test code should end up looking something like this:

ch3/src/Carousel.test.tsx
```
import { render, screen } from "@testing-library/react";
import userEvent from "@testing-library/user-event";
import Carousel from "./Carousel";

describe("Carousel", () => {
  const slides = [
    {
      imgUrl: "https://example.com/slide1.png",
      description: "Slide 1",
      attribution: "Uno Pizzeria",
    },
    {
      imgUrl: "https://example.com/slide2.png",
      description: "Slide 2",
      attribution: "Dos Equis",
    },
    {
```

```
          imgUrl: "https://example.com/slide3.png",
          description: "Slide 3",
          attribution: "Three Amigos",
      },
    ];

    it("renders a <div>", () => {
      render(<Carousel />);
      expect(screen.getByTestId("carousel")).toBeInTheDocument();
    });

    it("renders the first slide by default", () => {
      render(<Carousel slides={slides} />);
      const img = screen.getByRole("img");
      expect(img).toHaveAttribute("src", slides[0].imgUrl);
    });

    it("reverses the slide when the Prev button is clicked", async () => {
      render(<Carousel slides={slides} />);
      const img = screen.getByRole("img");
      const prevButton = screen.getByTestId("prev-button");
      const user = userEvent.setup();

      await user.click(prevButton);
      expect(img).toHaveAttribute("src", slides[2].imgUrl);
      await user.click(prevButton);
      expect(img).toHaveAttribute("src", slides[1].imgUrl);
      await user.click(prevButton);
      expect(img).toHaveAttribute("src", slides[0].imgUrl);
    });

    it("advances the slide when the Next button is clicked", async () => {
      render(<Carousel slides={slides} />);
      const img = screen.getByRole("img");
      const nextButton = screen.getByTestId("next-button");
      const user = userEvent.setup();

      await user.click(nextButton);
      expect(img).toHaveAttribute("src", slides[1].imgUrl);
      await user.click(nextButton);
      expect(img).toHaveAttribute("src", slides[2].imgUrl);
      await user.click(nextButton);
      expect(img).toHaveAttribute("src", slides[0].imgUrl);
    });
  });
```

And the component being tested should look like this:

ch3/src/Carousel.tsx
```tsx
import { ReactNode, useState } from "react";
import CarouselButton from "./CarouselButton";
import CarouselSlide from "./CarouselSlide";

type Slide = {
  imgUrl?: string;
  description?: ReactNode;
  attribution?: ReactNode;
};

const Carousel = ({ slides }: { slides?: Slide[] }) => {
  const [slideIndex, setSlideIndex] = useState(0);
  return (
    <div data-testid="carousel">
      <CarouselSlide {...slides?.[slideIndex]} />
      {}
      <CarouselButton
        data-testid="prev-button"
        onClick={() => {
          if (!slides) return;
          setSlideIndex((i) => (i + slides.length - 1) % slides.length);
        }}
      >
        Prev
      </CarouselButton>
      {}
      <CarouselButton
        data-testid="next-button"
        onClick={() => {
          if (!slides) return;
          setSlideIndex((i) => (i + 1) % slides.length);
        }}
      >
        Next
      </CarouselButton>
    </div>
  );
};

export default Carousel;
```

With that, this chapter's Carousel is complete! Put a bow on it with a commit:

```
:sparkles: Initial implementation of Carousel component
```

Mantra: Test One Piece at a Time

You've just built a complex component by coming up with a list of requirements and implementing those requirements in a TDD iteration loop. That allowed you to focus on one feature at a time without losing sight of the whole. You learned as you implemented each feature, and you carried that new knowledge into the next iteration of the loop. That's why this chapter's mantra is *Test one piece at a time.*

Now to recap. In this chapter, you learned how to write React code with the succinct JSX syntax along with TypeScript to typecheck that code. You set up ESLint to preemptively warn you about common React mistakes. Finally, you built a React carousel the TDD way, writing tests with Jest and React Testing Library for each piece of functionality you added.

In the next chapter, you'll add a much-needed coat of paint with styled-components, a unit-testable alternative to conventional style sheets.

CHAPTER 4

Styling in JavaScript with Styled-Components

Take a moment to consider the unlikely origins of the web as an app platform. When Tim Berners-Lee wrote the original web server and browser in 1990, web pages were written in a single language—HTML. HTML could only convey raw content; the way that content was presented was left to the browser. Gradually, a handful of stylistic choices were added to the markup language. Authors started to embellish their sites with (often garish) color and font choices, not to mention the infamous <marquee> tag. With the introduction of CSS in 1996, the aesthetic choices available to web designers exploded.

Around the same time that CSS was making headway, JavaScript began to bring interactivity to the web. The introduction of Gmail in 2004 proved that it was possible to build web apps that could rival their desktop counterparts, and with obvious advantages: no installation, instant updates, and access from any web-capable device. Developers flocked to the new platform. Since then, the three languages of the web—HTML, CSS, and JavaScript—have co-evolved, adding features to better complement each other. Miraculously, that evolution has allowed the web to compete with native app platforms even though none of its languages were invented with apps in mind.

Fast-forward to today. React has transformed web development by allowing developers to express the page's markup as a function of application state. But CSS remains largely static. In React apps that follow the tradition of keeping JavaScript and CSS separate, a layer of indirection is required in order to apply CSS rules based on application state: developers must write React components that render elements with particular class names based on their state, then write CSS rules for those class names to express the desired styles. As the list of CSS rules grow, developers inevitably struggle to keep them organized. The situation gets worse when components want to override the styles of other components they render, as "specificity wars" break out between the competing CSS rules.

Happily, many of these problems have a solution—CSS-in-JS, a paradigm exemplified by the popular styled-components library. With CSS-in-JS, you write styles using the familiar CSS syntax, but the actual style rules are generated at runtime as needed. This has enormous advantages for code organization and maintainability. And, not incidentally for the topic of this book, it also allows style rules to be subjected to unit tests.

In this chapter, you'll add styling to our carousel components from the previous chapter using styled-components. You'll make assertions about the components' styles using React Testing Library and capture them with Vitest's snapshots feature. But before you start styling, let's make some changes so that you can view your hard work from the last chapter in the browser.

Adding an Example Page

Open the test-driven-carousel project from the previous chapter and start the Vite dev server to serve the project to the browser:

```
$ npm run dev

  VITE v4.4.9  ready in 314 ms

  ➜  Local:   http://localhost:5173/
  ➜  Network: use --host to expose
  ➜  press h to show help
```

Open the URL shown in the output in your browser. You should be greeted by a blank page. Recall that you made the App component generated by Vite an empty placeholder, one that just returns null. Try making it render your Carousel component instead:

```
// src/App.tsx
import Carousel from "./Carousel";

export default function App() {
  return <Carousel />;
}
```

You should now see a pair of Prev and Next buttons. Since the carousel has no slides, these don't do much yet. So define an array of slides:

```
ch4/src/example/slides.tsx
const referralParams = "utm_source=test-driven-carousel&utm_medium=referral";

const getUsernameUrl = (username: string) =>
  `https://unsplash.com/@${username}?${referralParams}`;
```

```
const getAttribution = ({
  name,
  username,
}: {
  name: string;
  username: string;
}) => (
  <>
    Photo by <a href={getUsernameUrl(username)}>{name}</a> on{" "}
    <a href={`https://unsplash.com/?${referralParams}`}>Unsplash</a>
  </>
);

export default [
  {
    description: "Seattle",
    attribution: getAttribution({
      name: "Ganapathy Kumar",
      username: "gkumar2175",
    }),
    imgUrl:
      "https://images.unsplash.com/photo-1469321461812-afeb94496b27?w=1080" +
      "&ixid=eyJhcHBfaWQiOjIzODE4fQ&s=568095e79ee2cb55a795ad454ac9cf5e",
  },
  {
    description: "Chicago",
    attribution: getAttribution({
      name: "Austin Neill",
      username: "arstyy",
    }),
    imgUrl:
      "https://images.unsplash.com/photo-1484249170766-998fa6efe3c0?w=1080" +
      "&ixid=eyJhcHBfaWQiOjIzODE4fQ&s=f56c763ccf86e87644b049c9abbcf455",
  },
  {
    description: "Barcelona",
    attribution: getAttribution({
      name: "Enes",
      username: "royalfound",
    }),
    imgUrl:
      "https://images.unsplash.com/photo-1464790719320-516ecd75af6c?w=1080" +
      "&ixid=eyJhcHBfaWQiOjIzODE4fQ&s=e836c604036680eeba5c77ebdb171c73",
  },
  {
    description: "New York",
    attribution: getAttribution({
      name: "Anthony DELANOIX",
      username: "anthonydelanoix",
    }),
```

```
    imgUrl:
      "https://images.unsplash.com/photo-1423655156442-ccc11daa4e99?w=1080" +
      "&ixid=eyJhcHBfaWQiOjIzODE4fQ&s=54a272d03f5c06c416e8899f113dff06",
  },
  {
    description: "Rio de Janeiro",
    attribution: getAttribution({
      name: "Agustín Diaz",
      username: "agussdiaz28",
    }),
    imgUrl:
      "https://images.unsplash.com/photo-1483729558449-99ef09a8c325?w=1080" +
      "&ixid=eyJhcHBfaWQiOjIzODE4fQ&s=966003791f746c210b73863cf6170e6c",
  },
];
```

Using Unsplash Images

The images used in this book come from Unsplash,[a] a terrific resource for free photos. Please respect their guidelines.[b] Always accompany the photos with proper attribution, as the example application in this book does. If you want to use the photos in a different application, don't copy the URLs from this book. Instead, use the Unsplash API[c] to generate your own.

----

a.   https://unsplash.com/
b.   https://medium.com/unsplash/unsplash-api-guidelines-28e0216e6daa
c.   https://unsplash.com/developers

Then add an example component that wraps Carousel with those slides:

ch4/src/example/ExampleCarousel.tsx
```
import Carousel from "../Carousel";
import slides from "./slides";

export default function ExampleCarousel() {
  return <Carousel slides={slides} />;
}
```

Finally, plug that example component into the App component:

ch4/src/App.tsx
```
import ExampleCarousel from "./example/ExampleCarousel";

export default function App() {
  return <ExampleCarousel />;
}
```

Thanks to hot module reloading (HMR), your code changes should be served instantly to the browser by the Vite dev server, meaning there's no need to refresh. You should now see working slides in the carousel, on page 81.

Seattle Photo by Ganapathy Kumar on Unsplash

Prev   Next

Success! That's your carousel component, unstyled but fully functional. This is a good time for a commit, using the gitmoji for adding code documentation (there's one for everything!):

```
:bulb: Add example page
```

You're ready to start styling!

Getting Started with Styled-Components

As apps grow, they can contain thousands of style rules—too many for a single person to keep track of. This leads to unintended conflicts. For example, which of the styles below will apply to a disabled button with the white class?

```css
// StylesheetA.css
button.white {
  background-color: white;
  color: black;
}

// StylesheetB.css
button:disabled {
  background-color: grey;
  color: darkgrey;
}
```

The answer is that it depends on the order the style sheets are loaded in, as both selectors have the same level of specificity. This is a very fragile state of affairs for a complex app. Worse, removing style rules becomes a risky endeavor. Let's say that your app has this style rule:

```
p.alert-message {
  color: red;
}
```

You search your codebase for alert-message, find no results, and so you remove the style. But your search didn't match this React code:

```
<p className={`${urgency}-message`}>This is an alert!</p>
```

The CSS-in-JS paradigm, exemplified by a library called *styled-components*, greatly alleviates these problems by allowing a component's style rules to be written as a function of its props. This offers a number of advantages:

- No need to search your codebase to find out which styles are associated with a component. Its styles are either in the same module or imported like any other dependency.

- Styles are generated as a function of their component's props and state, just like markup.

- Styles can be subjected to unit tests.

And unlike the style prop, style rules generated by styled-components have the full range of functionality of ordinary CSS, including support for media queries, keyframe animations, and pseudo-classes.

Let's start adding some style to test-driven-carousel. Install the styled-components package as a dependency:

```
$ npm install --save styled-components@6.0.5
```

So far, this book's modus operandi has been to present tests first, then the code to satisfy these tests. This is, after all, a book about TDD, and TDD is usually taken to mean "writing tests first." But on a deeper level, TDD is about seeking useful feedback for your code as quickly as possible. Tests are just one possible source of feedback. And when it comes to styles, the most useful source of feedback is usually *seeing* those styles.

So set tests aside for now. All you'll need for this section is a live dev server.

Creating a Styled Component

Currently, the <img> created by CarouselSlide is unstyled, which means that it scales to whatever the original size of the image is. That means that the carousel jarringly expands and contracts as users move from slide to slide. Worse, it'll push other page content around in the process. Clearly, this needs to be fixed!

To do that, replace the unstyled <img> element with a component generated by styled-components:

```
// src/CarouselSlide.tsx
import { ComponentPropsWithRef, ReactNode } from "react";
import styled from "styled-components";

const ScaledImg = styled.img`
  object-fit: cover;
  width: 100%;
  height: 500px;
`;

const CarouselSlide = ({
  imgUrl,
  description,
  attribution,
  ...rest
}: {
  imgUrl?: string;
  description?: ReactNode;
  attribution?: ReactNode;
} & ComponentPropsWithRef<"figure">) => (
  <figure {...rest}>
    <ScaledImg src={imgUrl} />
    <figcaption data-testid="caption">
      <strong>{description}</strong> {attribution}
    </figcaption>
  </figure>
);

export default CarouselSlide;
```

styled.img is a function that generates a component that renders an <img> tag with the given styles. When an instance of that ScaledImg component is mounted, styled-components will dynamically insert a style rule with the styles you provided, using a class name selector based on the hash of those styles.

You'll see some syntactic fanciness here in the form of an ES6 feature called *tagged templates*:[1] if you put a function directly in front of a template string (the kind delimited by backticks), that function is called with the template string as an argument.

In the case of ScaledImg, you could use the normal function call syntax, since the string with the styles is a constant. Where the tagged template syntax unlocks new possibilities is when the string has interpolations (the ${...} syntax): each piece of the interpolated string is passed in to the function as a separate argument. That gives the tag function the chance to process interpolated variables. As we'll soon see, styled-components takes advantage of this power.

As soon as you hit save, you should see the difference in your browser. Before, the size of the <img> tag was determined by the image file it loaded. Now, it takes up the full width of its container and has 500px of height. The object-fit: cover rule means that the image keeps its aspect ratio as it expands or contracts to those dimensions, getting clipped as needed.

Why 500px? Really, the height of the image should be determined by the app rendering the carousel component. So let's add an imgHeight prop to CarouselSlide to allow the component consumer to override the default image height:

```
// src/CarouselSlide.tsx
import { ComponentPropsWithRef, ReactNode } from "react";
import styled from "styled-components";

const DEFAULT_IMG_HEIGHT = "500px";

export type CarouselSlideProps = {
  imgUrl?: string;
  /** @default "500px" */
  imgHeight?: string | number;
  description?: ReactNode;
  attribution?: ReactNode;
} & ComponentPropsWithRef<"figure">;

type ImgComponentProps = {
  $height?: CarouselSlideProps["imgHeight"];
};

const ScaledImg = styled.img<ImgComponentProps>`
  object-fit: cover;
  width: 100%;
  height: ${(
    props
  ) =>
```

---

1.   https://developer.mozilla.org/en-US/docs/Web/JavaScript/Reference/Template_literals#Tagged_templates

```
➤        typeof props.$height === "number" ? `${props.$height}px` : props.$height};
➤    `;

    const CarouselSlide = ({
      imgUrl,
➤      imgHeight = DEFAULT_IMG_HEIGHT,
      description,
      attribution,
      ...rest
    }: CarouselSlideProps) => (
      <figure {...rest}>
        {}
➤        <ScaledImg src={imgUrl} $height={imgHeight} />
➤        {}
        <figcaption data-testid="caption">
          <strong>{description}</strong> {attribution}
        </figcaption>
      </figure>
    );

    export default CarouselSlide;
```

❶ The /** ... */ syntax denotes a JSDoc comment. These comments don't affect the behavior of the code or the typechecker, but they can provide useful contextual information to developers who are using your code, complementing the TypeScript types.

For example, in VS Code if you hover over the imgHeight in <CarouselSlide imgHeight={}>, the editor will show you both its TypeScript type and the associated JSDoc. Here the JSDoc comment indicates that the default value used if the imgHeight prop is not set is "500px".

❷ The ImgComponentProps type is used as a *type parameter* for the styled.img function. In this case, the type parameter indicates the set of props that the ScaledImg component returned by that function will be able to accept, in addition to everything the native img tag can accept. The $ prefix in $height is a styled-components convention that indicates a *transient prop*, which is used for interpolated styles but not passed through to the <img> element in the DOM.

❸ This is where styled-components really gets exciting—interpolated values in the style template can be a function of the component's props! Whereas ordinary CSS is static, these styles are completely dynamic. If the imgHeight prop changes, the styles update automatically.

Right now, imgHeight can be overridden on a slide-by-slide basis, since Carousel passes the whole slide data object down to CarouselSlide as props. But in most cases, the Carousel consumer will want it to have a consistent height. So let's add a prop to Carousel that can override the default imgHeight on CarouselSlide:

```
// src/Carousel.tsx
import { ReactNode, useState } from "react";
import CarouselButton from "./CarouselButton";
import CarouselSlide, { CarouselSlideProps } from "./CarouselSlide";

type Slide = {
  imgUrl?: string;
  description?: ReactNode;
  attribution?: ReactNode;
};

export type CarouselProps = {
  slides: Slide[];
  defaultImgHeight?: CarouselSlideProps["imgHeight"];     ❶
};

const Carousel = ({ slides, defaultImgHeight }: CarouselProps) => {
  const [slideIndex, setSlideIndex] = useState(0);
  return (
    <div data-testid="carousel">
      <CarouselSlide imgHeight={defaultImgHeight} {...slides?.[slideIndex]} />   ❷
      {/* ... */}
    </div>
  );
};

export default Carousel;
```

❶ The CarouselSlideProps["imgHeight"] syntax references the type of the imgHeight field in CarouselSlideProps.

❷ Note that the order here is significant: because the ...slides?.[slideIndex] spread comes after imgHeight is set to defaultImgHeight, the imgHeight value from the slide will take precedence (if it's defined).

Try setting defaultImgHeight on ExampleCarousel, and you should see the carousel's height change in the browser.

Commit your work on this new feature:

```
:sparkles: Add image height styling
```

You may be wondering—how did styled-components apply those styles to the <img> tag? If you inspect one of the <img> tags in the browser, as in thescreenshot on page 87, you'll see that its class attribute is full of gobbledigook. Something like class="sc-bdVaJa hhfYDU". The styled-components library generated these class names for you and injected a corresponding style rule into a <style> tag in the <head> of the page.

In fact, the <img> element has two class names generated by styled-components. One of these, the one with the sc- prefix, is a stable class name that styled-components uses for selectors. The other, the one the styles are applied to, is generated from a hash of the styles. In practice, the distinction is just an implementation detail. Just remember: you should *never, ever* copy any class names generated by styled-components in your code! All generated class names are subject to change.

Having unreadable class names is an unfortunate drawback of styled-components. Luckily, it can be mitigated with help of a popular preprocessor, Babel.

Better Debugging with the Babel Plugin

Years before TypeScript hit the mainstream, the ubiquitous JavaScript preprocessor was Babel. At first, Babel was primarily used to transform code that used the latest ECMAScript features into code that could run in older browsers—even Internet Explorer! Then as React emerged, it also became the go-to way to compile JSX to JS. Today, TypeScript's built-in support for TSX, and its ability to compile to a specific ECMAScript target, has made Babel feel redundant to many developers. Fortunately, TypeScript and Babel can be used together, allowing TypeScript developers to tap into the enormous flexibility provided by Babel's plugin architecture.

Babel's powerful language-bending abilities can be used to tailor your code to the needs of specific libraries. That's what the official styled-components Babel plugin[2] does, enhancing styled-components code at compile time for better performance and easier debugging. It's a recommended addition for any project that uses styled-components.

Install the plugin with npm:

```
$ npm install --save-dev babel-plugin-styled-components@2.1.4
```

---

2. https://www.styled-components.com/docs/tooling#babel-plugin

Then add it to your Vite config like so, taking advantage of the fact that Vite's react plugin already uses Babel under the hood:

ch4/vite.config.ts
```
import { defineConfig } from "vitest/config";
import react from "@vitejs/plugin-react";

// https://vitejs.dev/config/
export default defineConfig({
  plugins: [
    react({
      babel: {
        plugins: [
          [
            "babel-plugin-styled-components",
            {
              displayName: true,
              fileName: true,
            },
          ],
        ],
      },
    }),
  ],
  test: {
    globals: true,
    environment: "happy-dom",
    setupFiles: ["test-setup.ts"],
  },
});
```

The Vite dev server should automatically restart when you change the configuration. Inspect the <img> element in the browser again:

Notice the difference? For one thing, the short class name has changed. (To reiterate—*never* copy class names generated by styled-components into your code!) But more importantly, the formerly sc- prefixed class name is now prefixed with CarouselSlide__ScaledImg-. Thanks to the Babel plugin, you can now see the module name (CarouselSlide) and component name (ScaledImg) associated with every element styled by styled-components! Note, however, that the short class name is still the one used as the style selector.

The Babel plugin also brings efficiency improvements, including the removal of comments and unnecessary whitespace from inside of your template literals, allowing you to write your styles in a human-friendly way without having to worry about the impact on your users' limited bandwidth.

Linting Styles with Stylelint

Once you're used to writing code with a powerful linter like ESLint, doing without a linter can feel like walking a highwire without a net—the slightest error can have dramatic effects! That applies to CSS just as it applies to JavaScript. One typo can ruin the look of an entire page. Worse, because browsers vary widely in how they interpret CSS syntax, malformed style rules may work as intended in your preferred development browser but spawn visual bugs in others.

Happily, it's possible to use the popular Stylelint[3] CSS linter on styles written for styled-components. Since ESLint ignores the contents of those template literals, the two linters have no trouble peacefully coexisting. In fact, they go together like chocolate and peanut butter.

You'll need a few packages for this: stylelint itself, stylelint-processor-styled-components to tell Stylelint which parts of the file to read, stylelint-config-standard to enable a reasonable set of default rules,[4] and postcss-styled-syntax to tell Stylelint how to parse styles within JavaScript/TypeScript files. Install them as dev dependencies:

```
$ npm install --save-dev stylelint@15.10.2 \
    stylelint-config-standard@34.0.0 \
    postcss-styled-syntax@0.4.0
```

Then create a .stylelintrc.js file in the project root:

```
ch4/.stylelintrc.cjs
module.exports = {
  extends: ["stylelint-config-standard"],
  customSyntax: "postcss-styled-syntax",
  allowEmptyInput: true,
};
```

And as with ESLint, you'll want to tell the linter to ignore the dist dir:

```
ch4/.stylelintignore
dist
```

---

3.   https://github.com/stylelint/stylelint
4.   https://github.com/stylelint/stylelint-config-standard

One more step—add stylelint to the project's lint and format scripts. Since we want it to look at TypeScript files (which have the extensions .ts or .tsx), the relevant command is stylelint "**/*.{ts,tsx}". To keep the line length in package.json manageable, split the script into two parts. Call the existing script lint:js, call the stylelint script lint:css, and run them both from the lint script. Then do the same with the format script:

```
...
"scripts": {
  "dev": "vite",
  "lint:js": "eslint . && prettier --list-different .",
  "lint:css": "stylelint \"**/*.{ts,tsx}\"",
  "lint": "npm run lint:js && npm run lint:css",
  "format:js": "eslint --fix . && prettier --loglevel warn --write .",
  "format:css": "stylelint \"**/*.{ts,tsx}\" --fix",
  "format": "npm run format:js && npm run format:css",
  "build": "tsc && vite build",
  "test": "vitest",
  "preview": "vite preview"
},
...
```

There should be no output (aside from npm's) if you run the script, indicating that everything is copacetic right now:

```
$ npm run lint
```

Try removing a semicolon from the styles in CarouselSlide.tsx, and you'll see how helpful Stylelint can be:

```
$ npm run lint
src/CarouselSlide.tsx
 15:20  ✖  Missed semicolon  CssSyntaxError

1 problem (1 error, 0 warnings)
```

If you're using VS Code, you'll want to install the official Stylelint extension[5] to automatically lint as you type.

From now on, any style code you write will enjoy the benefits of linter coverage. Make a commit:

```
:wrench: Initial stylelint setup
```

---

5.   https://marketplace.visualstudio.com/items?itemName=stylelint.vscode-stylelint

The Stylelint configuration here is just a starting point. For a complete list of rules supported by Stylelint that you might want to add to your project, check the official docs.[6]

Testing Styled Components

The carousel project's tests tell you that your components are rendering into the DOM the way you want, but those tests currently ignore the CSSOM (CSS Object Model), which determines the look and feel of all those DOM elements. The magic of styled-components is that it allows you to express styles as a function of props, which makes those styles ripe for testing.

In this section, you'll learn how to make assertions about styles in tests. You'll also learn how to expose a styled component to allow consumers to override its styles.

Making Assertions About Styles

To make assertions about the styles that styled-components generates, you'll need the Jest styled-components plugin.[7] Install jest-styled-components with npm:

```
$ npm install --save-dev jest-styled-components@7.1.1
```

Then you'll need to bring in the plugin before running your tests:

ch4/test-setup.ts
```
import "@testing-library/jest-dom/vitest";
➤ import "jest-styled-components";
```

Now you have a new assertion at your disposal, toHaveStyleRule(). Add a test to the describe("CarouselSlide") block to make sure that the expected styled.img styles are coming through:

```
// src/CarouselSlide.test.tsx
...
describe("CarouselSlide", () => {
  ...
➤  it("has the expected static styles", () => {
➤    render(<CarouselSlide />);
➤    const img = screen.getByRole("img");
➤    expect(img).toHaveStyleRule("object-fit", "cover");
➤    expect(img).toHaveStyleRule("width", "100%");
➤  });
});
```

---

6. https://stylelint.io/user-guide/rules/
7. https://github.com/styled-components/jest-styled-components

Those tests should all come through green. Now add another test to confirm that the imgHeight prop works as expected:

```
// src/CarouselSlide.test.tsx
...
describe("CarouselSlide", () => {
  ...
  it("uses `imgHeight` as the height of the <img>", () => {
    render(<CarouselSlide imgHeight="123px" />);
    expect(screen.getByRole("img")).toHaveStyleRule("height", "123px");
  });
});
```

Once again, all tests should be green. Time for a commit:

```
:white_check_mark: Add style tests for the <img>
```

Extending Styled Components

Now let's try out one of styled-components' coolest features. If you pass an existing styled component to styled(), it'll return a new component with the styles from the original component *plus* the new styles. The new styles take precedence, so this is a convenient way to override existing styles. In large projects, this approach offers an alternative to the "specificity wars" that ensue when style overrides are applied with higher-specificity CSS rules.

To start, modify CarouselSlide to add a new prop called ImgComponent, then export the ScaledImg component and use it as the default value of the new prop. In the render function, use <ImgComponent /> instead of <ScaledImg />.

```
ch4/src/CarouselSlide.tsx
import { ComponentPropsWithRef, ReactNode } from "react";
import styled from "styled-components";

const DEFAULT_IMG_HEIGHT = "500px";

export type CarouselSlideProps = {
  ImgComponent?: (
    props: ComponentPropsWithRef<"img"> & ImgComponentProps
  ) => JSX.Element;
  imgUrl?: string;
  /** @default "500px" */
  imgHeight?: string | number;
  description?: ReactNode;
  attribution?: ReactNode;
} & ComponentPropsWithRef<"figure">;

type ImgComponentProps = {
  $height?: CarouselSlideProps["imgHeight"];
};
```

```
export const ScaledImg = styled.img<ImgComponentProps>`
  object-fit: cover;
  width: 100%;
  height: ${(props) =>
    typeof props.$height === "number" ? `${props.$height}px` : props.$height};
`;

const CarouselSlide = ({
  ImgComponent = ScaledImg,
  imgUrl,
  imgHeight = DEFAULT_IMG_HEIGHT,
  description,
  attribution,
  ...rest
}: CarouselSlideProps) => (
  <figure {...rest}>
    {}
    <ImgComponent src={imgUrl} $height={imgHeight} />
    {}
    <figcaption data-testid="caption">
      <strong>{description}</strong> {attribution}
    </figcaption>
  </figure>
);

export default CarouselSlide;
```

Then add a test case that extends *StyledImg* with styled overrides and asserts
that the new styles are applied:

```
// src/CarouselSlide.test.tsx
import styled from "styled-components";
import { render, screen } from "@testing-library/react";
import CarouselSlide, { ScaledImg } from "./CarouselSlide";
...
describe("CarouselSlide", () => {
  ...
  it("allows styles to be overridden with `ImgComponent`", () => {
    const TestImg = styled(ScaledImg)`
      width: auto;
      object-fit: fill;
    `;
    render(<CarouselSlide ImgComponent={TestImg} imgHeight={250} />);
    expect(screen.getByRole("img")).toHaveStyleRule("width", "auto");
    expect(screen.getByRole("img")).toHaveStyleRule("height", "250px");
    expect(screen.getByRole("img")).toHaveStyleRule("object-fit", "fill");
  });
});
```

These tests should be green. Notice that the height property works the same way as it does on the original ScaledImg component, since TestImg doesn't override it.

Before the ImgComponent prop was added, the only way for the CarouselSlide consumer to alter the styles on the <img> element (aside from height) would've been to craft a CSS rule that targets it with an img element selector. But with the prop, the consumer can take the default component, extend it with new styles, and replace the original. Not only does that make it easy to override the styles, it also gives them a hook for inserting event handlers, DOM attributes, or additional markup—one prop, infinite extensibility!

As it stands, someone using Carousel who wants to modify <img> would have to set ImgComponent individually on each slide data object. It'd be convenient to be able to set a single prop on Carousel for modifying ImgComponent across the board, similar to the defaultImgHeight prop.

Let's switch back into TDD mode. Add some tests for both the as-yet-undefined DefaultImgComponent prop and the existing defaultImgHeight prop:

```
// src/Carousel.test.tsx
...
describe("Carousel", () => {
  ...
  it("passes DefaultImgComponent to the CarouselSlide", () => {
    const DefaultImgComponent = () => <img data-testid="Test image" />;
    render(
      <Carousel slides={slides} DefaultImgComponent={DefaultImgComponent} />
    );
    const img = screen.getByRole("img");
    expect(img).toHaveAttribute("data-testid", "Test image");
  });

  it("passes defaultImgHeight to the CarouselSlide", () => {
    const defaultImgHeight = 1234;
    render(<Carousel slides={slides} defaultImgHeight={defaultImgHeight} />);
    const img = screen.getByRole("img");
    expect(img).toHaveStyleRule("height", "1234px");
  });
});
```

Then move to the implementation:

```
ch4/src/Carousel.tsx
import { ReactNode, useState } from "react";
import CarouselButton from "./CarouselButton";
import CarouselSlide, { CarouselSlideProps } from "./CarouselSlide";
```

```
type Slide = {
  imgUrl?: string;
  description?: ReactNode;
  attribution?: ReactNode;
};

type CarouselProps = {
  slides?: Slide[];
  DefaultImgComponent?: CarouselSlideProps["ImgComponent"];
  defaultImgHeight?: CarouselSlideProps["imgHeight"];
};

const Carousel = ({
  slides,
  DefaultImgComponent,
  defaultImgHeight,
}: CarouselProps) => {
  const [slideIndex, setSlideIndex] = useState(0);
  return (
    <div data-testid="carousel">
      <CarouselSlide
        ImgComponent={DefaultImgComponent}
        imgHeight={defaultImgHeight}
        {...slides?.[slideIndex]}
      />
      <CarouselButton
        data-testid="prev-button"
        onClick={() => {
          if (!slides) return;
          setSlideIndex((i) => (i + slides.length - 1) % slides.length);
        }}
      >
        Prev
      </CarouselButton>
      <CarouselButton
        data-testid="next-button"
        onClick={() => {
          if (!slides) return;
          setSlideIndex((i) => (i + 1) % slides.length);
        }}
      >
        Next
      </CarouselButton>
    </div>
  );
};

export default Carousel;
```

And commit:

```
:sparkles: Add prop for extending the <img> component
```

At this point, let's pause and reflect on what it means to have adequate test coverage for styles. In this section, we created a toHaveStyleRule() assertion for every style rule. For dynamic rules like height, that's useful; anytime props are converted into something the user can see, it's worth making sure that conversion works as expected. But for static rules, toHaveStyleRule() is close to being a truism: "Test that x is x."

Still, it'd be nice to have some kind of sanity check when restyling components. What if you had a tool that automatically generated a diff of the component's styles before and after, allowing you to review and confirm that your changes reflect your intent? In the next section, you'll learn how to do just that using *snapshots*.

Taking Snapshots of Styles

When you think of testing, you probably picture a list of assertions about your code, a sort of checklist of its functionality. Up to this point, all of the tests in this book have fit that description. But sometimes a picture is worth a thousand words. Or in this case, a piece of content generated by your code can be worth a thousand assertions. Seeing a diff of that content can bring your attention to problems you might never have thought to write an assertion for.

That's the idea behind snapshots. When a test makes a snapshot assertion, it compares the content rendered in that test against a snapshot that was saved from a previous test run. If the assertion fails, you're presented with a diff and the option to update the snapshot, which would overwrite it with the new content. Snapshot tests are a convenient way to ensure that changes in your application's output go through human review.

For our purposes, the content we're interested in snapshotting is the DOM generated by CarouselSlide along with the styles generated by styled-components.

Now add a test with a new assertion, toMatchSnapshot():

```
// src/CarouselSlide.test.tsx
...
describe("CarouselSlide", () => {
  ...
  it("matches snapshot", () => {
    render(<CarouselSlide />);
    expect(screen.getByRole("figure")).toMatchSnapshot();
```

➤ ```
    });
  });
  ...
```

Then try running it:

```
$ npm test
 ✓ src/CarouselButton.test.tsx (3)
 ✓ src/CarouselSlide.test.tsx (9)
 ✓ src/Carousel.test.tsx (6)

  Snapshots  1 written
```

Vitest created a new directory, src/_snapshots_, with one file:

```
// src/__snapshots__/CarouselSlide.test.tsx.snap
// Vitest Snapshot v1, https://vitest.dev/guide/snapshot.html

exports[`CarouselSlide > matches snapshot 1`] = `
.c0 {
  object-fit: cover;
  width: 100%;
  height: 500px;
}

<figure>
  <img
    class="c0"
  />
  <figcaption data-testid="caption">
    <strong />

  </figcaption>
</figure>
`;
```

This snapshot provides a nice, clear picture of what CarouselSlide renders, including both the HTML markup and all of the style rules associated with it (by way of an autogenerated class name).

A snapshot like this is an excellent substitute for several of the existing tests about CarouselSlide's markup. Removing those rather rigid tests will help make it easier to change the component's markup and styles in the future; instead of making changes to multiple failing tests, you'll only have to confirm that the new snapshots reflect your intent.

Pruning the tests that are redundant with the snapshots yields the final CarouselSlide.test.tsx for this chapter:

ch4/src/CarouselSlide.test.tsx
```
import styled from "styled-components";
import { render, screen } from "@testing-library/react";
import CarouselSlide, { ScaledImg } from "./CarouselSlide";
```
```

```javascript
describe("CarouselSlide", () => {
  it("passes `imgUrl` through to the <img>", () => {
    const imgUrl = "https://example.com/image.png";
    render(<CarouselSlide imgUrl={imgUrl} />);
    expect(screen.getByRole("img")).toHaveAttribute("src", imgUrl);
  });

  it("uses `description` and `attribution` as the caption", () => {
    const props = {
      description: "A jaw-droppingly spectacular image",
      attribution: "Trevor Burnham",
    };
    render(<CarouselSlide {...props} />);
    const figcaption = screen.getByTestId("caption");
    expect(figcaption).toHaveTextContent(
      `${props.description} ${props.attribution}`
    );
  });

  it("passes other props through to the <figure>", () => {
    const props = {
      className: "my-carousel-slide",
      "data-test-name": "My slide",
    };
    render(<CarouselSlide {...props} />);
    const figure = screen.getByRole("figure");
    expect(figure).toHaveClass(props.className);
    expect(figure).toHaveAttribute("data-test-name", props["data-test-name"]);
  });

  it("uses `imgHeight` as the height of the <img>", () => {
    render(<CarouselSlide imgHeight="123px" />);
    expect(screen.getByRole("img")).toHaveStyleRule("height", "123px");
  });

  it("allows styles to be overridden with `ImgComponent`", () => {
    const TestImg = styled(ScaledImg)`
      width: auto;
      object-fit: fill;
    `;
    render(<CarouselSlide ImgComponent={TestImg} imgHeight={250} />);
    expect(screen.getByRole("img")).toHaveStyleRule("width", "auto");
    expect(screen.getByRole("img")).toHaveStyleRule("height", "250px");
    expect(screen.getByRole("img")).toHaveStyleRule("object-fit", "fill");
  });

  it("matches snapshot", () => {
    render(<CarouselSlide />);
    expect(screen.getByRole("figure")).toMatchSnapshot();
  });
});
```

From now on, every time you run your tests, Vitest will generate a new snapshot to compare to the old one. If the two are identical, the toMatchSnapshot() assertion passes. But what happens if they're different? Try changing, say, the object-fit style rule from cover to contain:

```
$ npm test
  FAIL  src/CarouselSlide.test.tsx > CarouselSlide > matches snapshot
Error: Snapshot `CarouselSlide > matches snapshot 1` mismatched
 > src/CarouselSlide.test.tsx:53:40
    51|   it("matches snapshot", () => {
    52|     render(<CarouselSlide />);
    53|     expect(screen.getByRole("figure")).toMatchSnapshot();
      |                                        ^
    54|   });
    55| });
  - Expected   - 1
  + Received   + 1
    `.c0 { ↵
  -   object-fit: cover; ↵
  +   object-fit: contain; ↵
```

When a toMatchSnapshot() assertion fails, Vitest treats that as a test failure and shows you a diff of the snapshot. The snapshot on disk remains unchanged. To confirm that your change is intentional, you would run the tests again with the -u (short for --updateSnapshot) flag, causing all snapshots to be overwritten. When running an npm command, flags passed to the underlying script need to be separated with --, so the complete command would be npm test -- -u.

> ### Snapshot Testing in Wallaby.js
>
> Wallaby offers excellent support for snapshot testing, including the ability to view snapshot diffs side-by-side in your editor and update snapshots individually. For details, check the official docs.[a] The docs for Jest apply equally to Vitest.
>
> _____
>
> a.   https://wallabyjs.com/docs/integration/jest.html#snapshot-testing

This snapshot process may feel strange at first. Unit tests are normally automated. Snapshot testing, by contrast, requires human intervention; on its own, the machine can't determine whether the test should pass or not. That brings human error into the equation. In practice, this downside is mitigated by the fact that snapshots are version controlled. If a pull request contains an unwanted change that's reflected in a snapshot that the author carelessly updated, everyone reviewing that pull request will see the snapshot diff and have a chance to raise a red flag.

Speaking of version control, it's time to make your final commit for this chapter:

```
:white_check_mark: Add snapshot tests for CarouselSlide
```

This concludes our tour of styled-components and testing. We only got around to styling one element, the <img>, so there's lots left to do! As an exercise for this chapter, try adding some finishing touches to the carousel. Play around with different styles for the caption, the buttons, and the overall layout. When you feel satisfied with your work, be sure to add a snapshot test for each element, then breathe a sigh of relief that your styles are safe from regressions.

Mantra: Actively Seek Feedback

The spirit of TDD extends beyond writing tests before you write code. The goal of TDD is to set up a constructive feedback loop for yourself, to identify potential problems quickly, and give yourself the freedom to explore potential improvements. Tests are only a means to that end. Sometimes, you'll want to set tests aside and focus on other sources of feedback. The important thing is to always think ahead: before you start writing a piece of code, ask yourself what the most valuable feedback you could receive for that code would be. Then take steps to make it a reality. In other words—*Actively seek feedback.*

In this chapter, you learned how to use the styled-components library to create components with integrated, extensible, fully testable styles. You also added some powerful new tools to your belt, including Stylelint and snapshot tests. Each of these tools give you more options for seeking feedback as you work. Whenever you find yourself stuck, ask if you might be focusing on the wrong kind of feedback.

In the next chapter, you'll learn how to write and test custom hooks to make React code reusable across multiple components.

Refactoring with Hooks

The power of React is that it allows you to express web apps in individual units called components. But the rules for assigning different bits of functionality to different components aren't always clear. In principle, any React app could be expressed as a single monolithic component. Or at the opposite extreme, every DOM element in the page could be managed by its own micro-component.

A good rule of thumb is that components should be built in such a way that each component has only one job. Components with multiple responsibilities are a good candidate for being split up. These distinctions are a matter of human intuition—no automated process is going to tell you whether a component has multiple responsibilities. Still, thinking in these terms will help you as you work to keep code manageable. The more complex an individual component is, the harder it'll be to make changes to it.

The first edition of this book recommended splitting up complex components into simpler pieces using a pattern called *higher-order components* (HOCs). However, the React ecosystem has evolved to offer an alternative: *hooks*. You'll use hooks to add new functionality to the carousel component from the previous chapter while actually streamlining the component's render function. And you'll learn how to use the React Devtools to debug components by inspecting their internal state.

Making Custom Hooks

Hooks are special functions that provide unique capabilities when called from a React component. For a complete list of those capabilities, see the React docs on hooks.[1]

---

1.   https://react.dev/reference/react

We've already used one hook, useState, which declares an internal state value. Let's take a closer look at that line in the Carousel component:

```
// src/Carousel.tsx
...
const [slideIndex, setSlideIndex] = useState(0);
...
```

The first time Carousel renders, the value of slideIndex is set to the value of the useState argument, 0. However, that argument is ignored in subsequent renders. Calling setSlideIndex tells React to update the slideIndex value and re-render the component. (As an optimization, React sometimes waits a moment to re-render the component so that multiple state updates will only trigger a single re-render.)

If you're paying close attention, you might wonder—how does React know *which* state to return when useState is called? After all, a single component could call the useState hook several times. The answer is that React relies on the order of hooks being the same every time a component is rendered. So when we call useState here, we're saying to React, "Give me the state corresponding to the first useState hook in this instance of Carousel." For that reason, it's important to avoid calling hooks conditionally or asynchronously.

Crucially, although the order in which a component calls hooks needs to be consistent, it doesn't matter whether those hooks are called directly from the component or indirectly through another function. And anytime we have a function that calls other hooks, that function *must* be treated like a hook, to preserve the order of the hooks it calls. We call that function a *custom hook*. By convention, custom hooks should have a name that starts with use, just like the hooks built into React.

Rules like "hooks must be called in the same order on every render" go against the grain of intuition. Thankfully, an official ESLint plugin can help guard against inadvertent violations of hook rules. Go ahead and install it before you get down to development:

```
$ npm install --save-dev eslint-plugin-react-hooks@4.6.0
```

Then add its recommended configuration to your ESLint config:

```
// .eslintrc.cjs
...
extends: [
  "eslint:recommended",
  "prettier",
  "plugin:react/recommended",
  "plugin:react/jsx-runtime",
```

```
    "plugin:testing-library/react",
➤   "plugin:react-hooks/recommended",
  ],
  ...
```

The linter plugin automatically applies rules to any function that follows the use* naming convention. Be sure to name your functions accordingly!

Now that those guardrails are in place, let's replace the useState call in Carousel with a custom hook called useSlideIndex. Start by creating a new file called useSlideIndex.tsx:

```
// src/useSlideIndex.tsx
import { useState } from "react";

export const useSlideIndex = () => {
  const [slideIndex, setSlideIndex] = useState(0);
  return [slideIndex, setSlideIndex] as const;
};
```

❶ The as const syntax here addresses a quirk of how TypeScript infers types on arrays. Without as const, TypeScript sees that the array returned by the function contains a number and a React.Dispatch<React.SetStateAction<number>>, so it infers the type of the array as (number | React.Dispatch<React.SetStateAction<number>>)[]. This means that every element in the array will match those types, but the array could have any number of those elements in any order!

The reason for this behavior is that TypeScript doesn't want to assume that the contents of the array will always match what the function returns. Arrays are mutable, after all. But in this case we have no intention of changing the array's contents. So we add as const to tell TypeScript to treat the array's contents as constant.

Then import it into Carousel.tsx and replace the existing useState call:

```
// src/Carousel.tsx
...
const [slideIndex, setSlideIndex] = useSlideIndex();
...
```

Run the tests to confirm that the behavior is unchanged.

So far this custom hook is trivial. But it gives us a place to put any component logic we want for the sake of code organization and code reuse. Let's try moving all of the logic related to the slide index into the hook.

In the component are two setSlideIndex calls, one for each button. Those click handlers are rather complicated, considering that all they do is decrement or increment the slide index. A good way to refactor this logic is to have the useSlideIndex hook return two functions called decrementSlideIndex and incrementSlideIndex, like so:

```
// src/useSlideIndex.tsx
import { useState } from "react";

export const useSlideIndex = (slides?: unknown[]) => {
  const [slideIndex, setSlideIndex] = useState(0);

  const decrementSlideIndex = () => {
    if (!slides) return;
    setSlideIndex((i) => (i + slides.length - 1) % slides.length);
  };
  const incrementSlideIndex = () => {
    if (!slides) return;
    setSlideIndex((i) => (i + 1) % slides.length);
  };

  return [slideIndex, decrementSlideIndex, incrementSlideIndex] as const;
};
```

❶ The unknown type in TypeScript allows anything to be assigned to it. Here it's used for convenience because slides is only being used as an array: we care whether it exists and what its length is but not about its individual values. Using unknown here saves us the trouble of exporting the Slide type from the Carousel module.

Then use the new hook functionality to simplify the component:

```
// src/Carousel.tsx
...
const Carousel = ({
  slides,
  DefaultImgComponent,
  defaultImgHeight,
}: CarouselProps) => {
  const [slideIndex, decrementSlideIndex, incrementSlideIndex] =
    useSlideIndex(slides);
  return (
    <div data-testid="carousel">
      <CarouselSlide
        ImgComponent={DefaultImgComponent}
        imgHeight={defaultImgHeight}
        {...slides?.[slideIndex]}
      />
      {}
      <CarouselButton data-testid="prev-button" onClick={decrementSlideIndex}>
        Prev
      </CarouselButton>
      <CarouselButton data-testid="next-button" onClick={incrementSlideIndex}>
        Next
      </CarouselButton>
```

```
      {}
    </div>
  );
};
...
```

Run the tests to make sure the refactoring preserved the Prev/Next button functionality. They should still be green. This is a perfect example of how unit tests allow refactoring to be done quickly and confidently!

Commit your work so far, using the :recycle: gitmoji to indicate a refactoring:

```
:recycle: Refactor Carousel with useSlideIndex hook
```

In the next section, you'll make this custom hook even more powerful by adding the ability for the component consumer to control the slide index.

The Controllable Pattern

Components in React are commonly described as either *controlled* or *uncontrolled* with respect to some variable. If that variable is passed down to it through props, the component is controlled. If that variable is managed as state, the component is uncontrolled.

As it stands, Carousel is uncontrolled with respect to slideIndex. That's convenient for consumers, since they don't have to implement the Prev/Next button logic themselves. However, it limits the flexibility of the component. For example, the component consumer might want to render a Reset button that takes the user back to the first slide, but they can't do that if the slide index only exists in state.

What if you could get the best of both worlds? That's what the *controllable* pattern offers. As its name suggests, a controllable component is one that can be optionally controlled. If the user chooses not to control the variable in question, then it functions as an uncontrolled component. The controllable pattern is exemplified by React's own form elements, for example <input>.

In this section, you'll modify useSlideIndex to make the slideIndex on Carousel controllable.

Making Carousel controllable entails accepting slideIndex and onSlideIndexChange props with the following behavior:

- If the slideIndex prop is undefined, it continues to function the way it always has, changing its slideIndex state internally when the Prev/Next buttons are clicked.

- If the slideIndex prop is defined, it overrides the internal state. To make the Prev/Next buttons work, the consumer will need to pass in an onSlideIndex-Change prop to listen for cases where the component would change its internal state, and update the slideIndex prop it passes in accordingly. React components have no power to update their own props.

This set of requirements is a great candidate for unit testing. It's worth asking—should these tests be written against the Carousel component or directly against the useSlideIndex hook? Writing tests against hooks is definitely an option, and there's even a library for that purpose, react-hooks-testing-library.[2] However, it usually feels more natural to write tests against components. All of the requirements listed are easily expressible as tests against the Carousel component, so let's go with that approach.

The existing tests cover the uncontrolled pattern well, so all you need to do is add test cases for the controlled pattern. Add a new describe block outlining the expected behavior when the slideIndex prop is set:

```
// Carousel.test.tsx
...
describe("with controlled slideIndex", () => {
  const onSlideIndexChange = vi.fn();
  const renderCarouselWithSlideIndex = () =>
    render(
      <Carousel
        slides={slides}
        slideIndex={1}
        onSlideIndexChange={onSlideIndexChange}
      />
    );

  beforeEach(() => {
    onSlideIndexChange.mockReset();
  });

  it("shows the slide corresponding to slideIndex", () => {
    renderCarouselWithSlideIndex();
    const img = screen.getByRole("img");
    expect(img).toHaveAttribute("src", slides[1].imgUrl);
  });

    it("calls onSlideIndexChange when Prev is clicked", async () => {
    renderCarouselWithSlideIndex();
    const img = screen.getByRole("img");
    const prevButton = screen.getByTestId("prev-button");
    const user = userEvent.setup();

    await user.click(prevButton);
```

---

2.   https://react-hooks-testing-library.com/

```
③      expect(img).toHaveAttribute("src", slides[1].imgUrl); // no change
④      expect(onSlideIndexChange).toHaveBeenCalledWith(0);
     });

     it("calls onSlideIndexChange when Next is clicked", async () => {
       renderCarouselWithSlideIndex();
       const img = screen.getByRole("img");
       const nextButton = screen.getByTestId("next-button");
       const user = userEvent.setup();

       await user.click(nextButton);
       expect(img).toHaveAttribute("src", slides[1].imgUrl); // no change
       expect(onSlideIndexChange).toHaveBeenCalledWith(2);
     });
   });
   ...
```

❶ vi.fn() creates a mock function which tracks calls to itself, allowing you to
write assertions about those calls. If you're coming to Vitest from Jest,
you may recognize it as the equivalent of jest.fn().

❷ By default, mocks preserve their state across tests, which is usually
undesirable. The mockReset method resets the mock to be as good as new.

❸ This assertion verifies that the carousel's internal logic has no effect on
which slide is shown when slideIndex is controlled with a prop.

❹ toHaveBeenCalledWith is a standard matcher in both Jest and Vitest. The
assertion succeeds if the function has been called with the given list of
arguments, and fails otherwise. Note that this assertion will only work
for mock functions.

Now, to turn these tests from red to green will require changes to both the
hook and the component. Let's start with the hook, which contains the core
logic for the controllable functionality:

```
// src/useSlideIndex.tsx
import { useState } from "react";

const decrement = (length: number) =>
①  (i: number) => (i + length - 1) % length;
const increment = (length: number) =>
   (i: number) => (i + 1) % length;

export const useSlideIndex = (
  slides?: unknown[],
  slideIndexProp?: number,
  onSlideIndexChange?: (newSlideIndex: number) => void
) => {
  const [slideIndexState, setSlideIndexState] = useState(0);

  // Controllable pattern: The prop takes precedence over the state.
```

```
❷   const slideIndex = slideIndexProp ?? slideIndexState;

    const decrementSlideIndex = () => {
      if (!slides) return;
      setSlideIndexState(decrement(slides.length));
❸     onSlideIndexChange?.(decrement(slides.length)(slideIndex));
    };
    const incrementSlideIndex = () => {
      if (!slides) return;
      setSlideIndexState(increment(slides.length));
      onSlideIndexChange?.(increment(slides.length)(slideIndex));
    };

    return [slideIndex, decrementSlideIndex, incrementSlideIndex] as const;
};
```

❶ The decrement and increment functions here are written using a technique called *currying*, which is when a function takes a value and returns another function that uses that value. That way, the function returned by decrement(length)/increment(length) can be used as a state setter.

❷ The ?? is the *nullish coalescing operator*. It returns the left-hand value if that value is neither undefined nor null. Otherwise, it returns the right-hand value.

Note that the more common slideIndexProp || slideIndexState syntax wouldn't do what we want here: if slideIndexProp were 0, it would fail to take precedence over slideIndexState.

❸ You've seen the optional chaining syntax ?. used for property access before. Here the same syntax is being used for a function call: onSlideIndexChange is called if, and only if, it's defined.

Then we'll change the component, which just needs to be modified to accept the new props and pass them through to the hook:

```
// src/Carousel.tsx
...
type CarouselProps = {
  slides?: Slide[];
➤   slideIndex?: number;
❶   onSlideIndexChange?: (newSlideIndex: number) => void;
  DefaultImgComponent?: CarouselSlideProps["ImgComponent"];
  defaultImgHeight?: CarouselSlideProps["imgHeight"];
};

const Carousel = ({
  slides,
❷   slideIndex: slideIndexProp,
➤   onSlideIndexChange,
  DefaultImgComponent,
```

```
      defaultImgHeight,
    }: CarouselProps) => {
➤     const [slideIndex, decrementSlideIndex, incrementSlideIndex] =
➤       useSlideIndex(
➤         slides,
➤         slideIndexProp,
➤         onSlideIndexChange
➤       );
      ...
```

❶ This type says that the onSlideIndexChange function can be any function that accepts a single number as its argument. The argument name, newSlideIndex, doesn't matter to the typechecker, only to humans looking at these types as documentation. The return type, void, tells TypeScript that we don't care about the function's return value.

❷ The slideIndex: slideIndexProp syntax here means "Give me the slideIndex prop, but assign it to a variable named slideIndexProp." It's a good practice to use this naming convention when there's the potential for confusion between props and state.

Run the tests to verify that the new functionality is working smoothly. Once the tests are green, it's time to commit your work:

```
:sparkles: Allow the slideIndex in Carousel to be controlled
```

Congratulations on writing your first controllable component! The controllable pattern is often a challenge for React component authors to get right. Happily, you have solid tests in place to prove that you did.

In the next section, you'll add one more feature that involves a tricky concept for testing: time.

Testing with Timers

As we've seen, you can use hooks within hooks as long as you follow the rules of hooks every step of the way. That extends to custom hooks as well.

In this section, you'll add a new feature to Carousel: the ability to auto-advance the slideIndex on Carousel every few seconds with a timer. To keep useSlideIndex from becoming too big and complex, the timer logic will be encapsulated in a new custom hook used within useSlideIndex.

But before getting to the implementation, let's write some tests.

Using Fake Timers in Tests

Testing code that uses timers poses an obvious problem: how do you write tests that give you instant feedback if you need to wait for timers to resolve? The answer is, you don't. Modern test frameworks have solved this problem by offering *fake timers*. When enabled, fake timers replace setTimeout, setInterval, and other built-in timing functions with functions that you control, allowing you to simulate the passage of any amount of time in the blink of an eye.

In Vitest, you enable fake timers by calling vi.useFakeTimers() and switch back to real timers by calling vi.useRealTimers(). For our purposes, it makes more sense to use fake timers consistently, so go ahead and add this line to your test setup code:

```
ch5/test-setup.ts
import "@testing-library/jest-dom/vitest";
import "jest-styled-components";

➤ vi.useFakeTimers();
```

If you try and run your tests after making this change, you'll notice something alarming—all of your tests with click handlers are failing! This is due to a bug (unresolved as of this writing)[3] with testing-library's simulated user events. It uses native timer functions to simulate the asynchronous nature of DOM events and currently fails to recognize when Vitest has replaced those functions. Thankfully we can work around this bug by setting an option called shouldAdvanceTime on Vitest's fake timers:

```
ch5/vite.config.ts
import { defineConfig } from "vitest/config";
import react from "@vitejs/plugin-react";

// https://vitejs.dev/config/
export default defineConfig({
  plugins: [
    react({
      babel: {
        plugins: [
          [
            "babel-plugin-styled-components",
            {
              displayName: true,
              fileName: true,
            },
          ],
```

---

3. https://github.com/testing-library/react-testing-library/issues/1197

```
        ],
      },
    }),
  ],
  test: {
    globals: true,
    environment: "happy-dom",
    setupFiles: ["test-setup.ts"],
    // Workaround for testing-library/react-testing-library#1197
    fakeTimers: { shouldAdvanceTime: true },
  },
});
```

With that change, all tests should be in the green again. Now to write the test for the auto-advance functionality! To simulate the passage of time, just call vi.advanceTimersByTime(duration), where duration is in milliseconds (just like the argument you'd pass to setTimeout).

One more important note—you'll need to wrap the advance timer call in a special function called act, which you can import from @testing-library/react. The act function tells React, "I've made some changes to component state and I want to make sure those changes are flushed to the DOM." If you ever make state changes without act, you'll see a warning about it in the test output.

User Events and act

When learning about act, you might wonder—why didn't you need act before, when you were simulating clicks? Didn't that also change component state?

The answer is, you did! As a convenience, testing-library's user-event package wraps its interactions with act for you. But Vitest's timer advancement functions don't, so you need to wrap them with act yourself.

Here's what the new test might look like:

```
// src/Carousel.test.tsx
...
describe("with auto-advance", () => {
  it("advances the slide according to autoAdvanceInterval", () => {
    const autoAdvanceInterval = 5_000;
    render(
      <Carousel slides={slides} autoAdvanceInterval={autoAdvanceInterval} />
    );
    const img = screen.getByRole("img");
    expect(img).toHaveAttribute("src", slides[0].imgUrl);

    act(() => {
      vi.advanceTimersByTime(autoAdvanceInterval);
    });
```

```
    expect(img).toHaveAttribute("src", slides[1].imgUrl);

    act(() => {
      vi.advanceTimersByTime(autoAdvanceInterval);
    });
    expect(img).toHaveAttribute("src", slides[2].imgUrl);
  });
});
...
```

Now you have a test in place for the auto-advance feature. To implement that functionality, you'll need to use a hook we haven't seen yet: useEffect.

Setting Timers with the useEffect Hook

React offers several hooks, but the two most important are useState (which we've seen) and useEffect. The purpose of useEffect is to schedule code to run outside of the render function. For the auto-advance feature, it wouldn't make sense to set a timer every time the component renders. We only want to set the timer when the component first mounts, when the slide has advanced, and maybe when the autoAdvanceInterval prop changes.

Let's write a general-purpose hook to set a timeout with useEffect. We'll call it useTimeout. Here's an implementation:

```
ch5/src/useTimeout.tsx
import { useEffect } from "react";

export const useTimeout = (
  delay: number | undefined,
  callback: () => void
) => {
❶  useEffect(() => {
    if (!delay) return;
❷    const timeout = setTimeout(callback, delay);
❸    return () => {
      clearTimeout(timeout);
    };
❹  }, [delay, callback]);
};
```

❶ The first argument to useEffect is a function that produces the effect you want. The function always runs after the component's first render. Depending on the second argument, it may run after other renders, as explained in the following text.

❷ setTimeout is a standard JavaScript function that calls the given callback after the given number of milliseconds. It also returns a handle that can be passed to clearTimeout.

❸ You can optionally return another function from your effect function. This function is typically used for cleanup; it's invoked before the effect function is called after subsequent renders and also before the component unmounts. Here it's being used to cancel any pending timeout.

❹ The second argument to useEffect is an array of dependencies. Every time the component renders, React will compare these dependencies to their previous values and invoke the effect function only if they've changed.

Putting it all together, this useEffect says, "If delay is a non-zero number, set a timeout to run callback after delay. If delay or callback changes, clear the timeout and set a new one. Oh, and clear the timeout when the component unmounts." Considering all that logic, this hook is quite succinct! That's the beauty of hooks.

With this new hook, implementing the auto-advance feature should be a breeze. Modify useSlideIndex to accept an autoAdvanceInterval argument and pass it through to useTimeout:

```
// src/useSlideIndex.ts
import { useState } from "react";
➤ import { useTimeout } from "./useTimeout";

const decrement = (length: number) =>
  (i: number) => (i + length - 1) % length;
const increment = (length: number) =>
  (i: number) => (i + 1) % length;

export const useSlideIndex = (
  slides?: unknown[],
  slideIndexProp?: number,
  onSlideIndexChange?: (newSlideIndex: number) => void,
➤  autoAdvanceInterval?: number
) => {
  ...

➤  useTimeout(autoAdvanceInterval, incrementSlideIndex);

  return [slideIndex, decrementSlideIndex, incrementSlideIndex] as const;
};
```

At first glance, this may look like it would only auto-advance once. But remember that the callback, namely incrementSlideIndex, is a dependency of the useEffect function. And incrementSlideIndex is actually a different function every time the slide changes. So after the slide changes, a new timeout is set. As a result, the auto-advance will work continuously. (You may notice that there's a subtle flaw in this callback dependency logic. We'll revisit it in the next section.)

Finally, plug in the new autoAdvanceInterval prop in the Carousel component:

```tsx
ch5/src/Carousel.tsx
import { ReactNode } from "react";
import CarouselButton from "./CarouselButton";
import CarouselSlide, { CarouselSlideProps } from "./CarouselSlide";
import { useSlideIndex } from "./useSlideIndex";

type Slide = {
  imgUrl?: string;
  description?: ReactNode;
  attribution?: ReactNode;
};

type CarouselProps = {
  slides?: Slide[];
  slideIndex?: number;
  onSlideIndexChange?: (newSlideIndex: number) => void;
  autoAdvanceInterval?: number;
  DefaultImgComponent?: CarouselSlideProps["ImgComponent"];
  defaultImgHeight?: CarouselSlideProps["imgHeight"];
};

const Carousel = ({
  slides,
  slideIndex: slideIndexProp,
  onSlideIndexChange,
  autoAdvanceInterval,
  DefaultImgComponent,
  defaultImgHeight,
}: CarouselProps) => {
  const [slideIndex, decrementSlideIndex, incrementSlideIndex] = useSlideIndex(
    slides,
    slideIndexProp,
    onSlideIndexChange,
    autoAdvanceInterval
  );
  return (
    <div data-testid="carousel">
      <CarouselSlide
        ImgComponent={DefaultImgComponent}
        imgHeight={defaultImgHeight}
        {...slides?.[slideIndex]}
      />
      <CarouselButton data-testid="prev-button" onClick={decrementSlideIndex}>
        Prev
      </CarouselButton>
      <CarouselButton data-testid="next-button" onClick={incrementSlideIndex}>
        Next
      </CarouselButton>
    </div>
  );
```

```
};
export default Carousel;
```

Run the tests again, and voilà! You should be in the green. Go ahead and commit the new feature:

```
:sparkles: Add auto-advance support to Carousel
```

In the next section, we'll look more closely at the useEffect dependency logic and fix a bug in it using another hook, useCallback.

Preventing Unnecessary Updates with useCallback and useRef

In the last section, I mentioned that useTimeout(autoAdvanceInterval, incrementSlideIndex) will keep advancing the slide forever because each time the slide advances, a new incrementSlideIndex function is generated. That's true, but there's a problem—any other re-render will also generate a new incrementSlideIndex function! When that happens, our timeout will be reset.

To demonstrate the problem, here's a test case where we trigger a re-render in Carousel right before the auto-advance timeout would trigger:

```
// src/Carousel.test.tsx
...
it("does not reset the auto-advance timer on re-render", () => {
  const autoAdvanceInterval = 5_000;
  const { rerender } = render(
    <Carousel slides={slides} autoAdvanceInterval={autoAdvanceInterval} />
  );
  const img = screen.getByRole("img");
  expect(img).toHaveAttribute("src", slides[0].imgUrl);

  act(() => {
    vi.advanceTimersByTime(autoAdvanceInterval - 1);
  });
  expect(img).toHaveAttribute("src", slides[0].imgUrl);

  rerender(
    <Carousel slides={slides} autoAdvanceInterval={autoAdvanceInterval} />
  );

  act(() => {
    vi.advanceTimersByTime(1);
  });
  expect(img).toHaveAttribute("src", slides[1].imgUrl);
});
...
```

This test is in the red. But why? Here's a step-by-step run-through:

1. Re-rendering Carousel causes useSlideIndex to be called. It generates a new incrementSlideIndex, which gets passed through to useTimeout, which uses it as the callback dependency in useEffect.

2. React sees that the callback dependency changed. First it runs the cleanup function, clearing the existing timeout. Then it runs the effect function to set a new one. The fact that the new callback dependency is equivalent to the old one is irrelevant; React only does exact === comparisons, so any new function or object will register as changed.

As a result, even though you've already waited 4.999 seconds, you'd have to wait another 5 seconds for the effect to fire! This may seem like an edge case, but it's very common for re-renders to propagate this way in React. You have to be ready for them.

One way to mitigate this problem is to use React's memo function[4] to make your component re-render conditionally. Using memo, you could prevent Carousel from re-rendering when its parent re-renders but passes in the same props. memo is a great optimization, but preventing unnecessary Carousel re-renders wouldn't completely solve the problem here; Carousel could still re-render for reasons that have nothing to do with the slide index, such as if its parent component changes the defaultImgHeight or DefaultImgComponent props.

What we really need is a way to control when a new incrementSlideIndex function is generated. Thankfully, React provides a hook for exactly that purpose: useCallback.

Just like useEffect, the useCallback hook takes two arguments: a function and an array of dependencies. However, instead of executing the function, it returns it. And crucially, it returns the *same* function as long as the dependencies are unchanged. This is sometimes referred to as memoizing the function, though that terminology is a bit confusing; usually when someone talks about memoizing a function, they're talking about caching the function's result. Here, the function itself is being cached.

Try wrapping the incrementSlideIndex function in useCallback, with all of the variables used in the function as dependencies:

```
// src/useSlideIndex.tsx
...
const incrementSlideIndex = useCallback(() => {
  if (!slides) return;
```

4. https://react.dev/reference/react/memo

```
  setSlideIndexState(increment(slides.length));
  onSlideIndexChange?.(increment(slides.length)(slideIndex));
}, [slides, slideIndex, onSlideIndexChange]);
...
```

Now incrementSlideIndex will be the same function as long as slides, slideIndex, and onSlideIndexChange remain the same. And with that, the re-render test now passes!

> ## The Exhaustive Deps Rule
>
> You may notice that if you don't pass in all three dependencies to useCallback, eslint-plugin-react-hooks will emit a warning mentioning the missing dependency. This react-hooks/exhaustive-deps rule is somewhat controversial because in some scenarios it's reasonable to omit dependencies. For example, you may want an effect to only run on mount, using the initial props to perform some initialization. In that case, the correct dependency array would be [].
>
> However, omitting dependencies by accident is a common source of bugs. So my advice is to keep the linter rule enabled and use a comment like this to override the rule when you need to:
>
> `// eslint-disable-next-line react-hooks/exhaustive-deps`
>
> Be sure to add a separate comment explaining your reasoning. Future readers of your code will thank you!

We still have a problem with this dependency logic, though: if the parent component isn't careful about caching the slides or onSlideIndexChange values across re-renders, we're going to get the same problem we were having without useCallback. This is a common problem in React. It's easy for a developer to declare slides or onSlideIndexChange inline without realizing that it could create different behavior than reusing the same values would.

Here's another test case to demonstrate:

```
// src/Carousel.test.tsx
...
it("does not reset the timer on irrelevant prop changes", () => {
  const autoAdvanceInterval = 5_000;
  const CarouselParent = () => (
    <Carousel
      slides={[...slides]}
      onSlideIndexChange={vi.fn()}
      autoAdvanceInterval={autoAdvanceInterval}
    />
  );
  const { rerender } = render(<CarouselParent />);
  const img = screen.getByRole("img");
  expect(img).toHaveAttribute("src", slides[0].imgUrl);
```

```
  act(() => {
    vi.advanceTimersByTime(autoAdvanceInterval - 1);
  });
  expect(img).toHaveAttribute("src", slides[0].imgUrl);

  rerender(<CarouselParent />);

  act(() => {
    vi.advanceTimersByTime(1);
  });
  expect(img).toHaveAttribute("src", slides[1].imgUrl);
});
...
```

Every time CarouselParent renders, slides is a new array and onSlideIndexChange is a new function, so the useCallback hook registers those dependencies as changed, preventing it from working as intended.

What can we do about this? The simplest fix would be to remove slides and onSlideIndexChange from the dependency array. However, that would introduce potential bugs when the incrementSlideIndex function references the old versions of those props. So let's think carefully about how these dependencies are used:

1. We only use slides to determine the bounds of slideIndex so that incrementing past the last slide will wrap around to the first slide. That means that we don't really care if slides itself changes, as long as slides.length is the same.

2. We always want to call the latest onSlideIndexChange function, but we don't want changes in that prop to have secondary effects. That suggests that we should store a reference to onSlideIndexChange somewhere outside of incrementSlideIndex.

Seen that way, the slides problem is an easy fix. Simply replace the two references to slides with slides.length—or rather, with slides?.length, since slides could be undefined:

```
// src/useSlideIndex.tsx
...
const incrementSlideIndex = useCallback(() => {
➤   if (!slides?.length) return;
    setSlideIndexState(increment(slides.length));
    onSlideIndexChange?.(increment(slides.length)(slideIndex));
➤ }, [slides?.length, slideIndex, onSlideIndexChange]);
...
```

As to the onSlideIndexChange dependency, another React hook is made for exactly this purpose—useRef. It's the simplest hook, taking an initial value as its argument and returning an object of the form {current: value}. After the first render, that argument is ignored and the same object is returned without modification. You can set current to whatever you want, whenever you want, without triggering re-renders.

Try using useRef to store a reference to the latest onSlideIndexChange and then calling the ref value from incrementSlideIndex:

```
// src/useSlideIndex.tsx
...
// Store a reference to onSlideIndexChange to avoid dependency issues.
const onSlideIndexChangeRef = useRef(onSlideIndexChange);
onSlideIndexChangeRef.current = onSlideIndexChange;
...
const incrementSlideIndex = useCallback(() => {
  if (!slides?.length) return;
  setSlideIndexState(increment(slides.length));
  onSlideIndexChangeRef.current?.(increment(slides.length)(slideIndex));
}, [slides?.length, slideIndex]);
...
```

❶ The argument to useRef here doesn't matter, since this initial value is overwritten by the next line. However, it does allow TypeScript to infer the type of the ref object, which is a bit more convenient than setting the type explicitly.

❷ You don't need to declare onSlideIndexChangeRef as a dependency. If you were to declare it, it wouldn't have any effect, because it's always the same object. Only its current value changes.

With those changes, the tests should all be in the green! Commit your patch for the now thoroughly tested auto-advance feature:

```
:bug: Prevent updates from resetting auto-advance timer
```

That concludes the coding portion of this chapter. You've successfully used hooks for both refactoring and keeping new features in isolation, preventing complexity sprawl. Before the chapter concludes, we'll take a brief look at the components you've built from another angle.

Inspecting Components with React Devtools

Refactoring components with hooks has the advantage of keeping code in manageable units, but as those units grow in number, it's easy to lose track of how they all fit together. One way to regain perspective is to take a look at the components in action through the React Developer Tools.[5]

---

5. https://react.dev/learn/react-developer-tools

Install the React Devtools in your browser of choice (or if you're using Safari, use the stand-alone react-devtools as explained in the docs). Open the Carousel test page, then navigate to the React panel that the extension added to the developer console. You'll get a nice view of the entire tree of React components on the page along with their props and state, as shown in the following screenshot.

You can quickly locate any component you're interested in, using the search bar. Click a component in the tree, and the selected component's props and hooks will appear on the right side. The hooks are laid out in a neat tree that you can drill down into. You can even edit props and state values in real time and see what effects those changes will have.

This bird's-eye view is invaluable for debugging. Start with the component that's rendering the unexpected output—most likely, the problem is caused by a problematic prop value. Work your way up the tree to see which component is passing that prop in. Then you can write up a unit test against that component to describe the problem and quickly get it fixed.

Mantra: Keep the Unit Small

As applications grow in size, they grow more difficult for humans to understand as a whole. That's unavoidable. However, there's also a tendency for individual parts of the codebase to become more difficult to reconcile with one another, for indirect and implicit connections to be created that go unnoticed until they're accidentally corrupted, causing bugs. And that tendency is avoidable. You can be vigilant about keeping each module small enough for its purpose to come across clearly; in testing terms, *Keep the unit small.*

In this chapter, you learned an important technique for keeping React components compact and purposeful: splitting layers of functionality into hooks. You turned what could have been a single unwieldy component into three simple, reusable ones. And you learned to use the React Devtools to get a picture of how your components fit together to create an entire app.

With that, you have all the concepts you need to be a first-rate React developer. The next and final chapter will return to tooling, this time with the goal of improving collaboration.

Continuous Integration and Collaboration

A recurring theme of this book has been the power of automation to improve your workflow. When properly applied, tools like ESLint and Jest greatly increase the chances that you'll catch mistakes in your code long before that code has a chance to go into production. But your workflow is just that—yours. When you're working as part of a team or maintaining an open source project, how do you extend the power of automation to your collaborators?

One answer is good old-fashioned documentation: "Please run the tests before submitting a patch." But that leaves the door open for human error. A better solution is to offload such quality control checks to a server, away from the personalized environments of developer machines. This technique has become known as continuous integration (CI).

Continuous integration takes weight off of your shoulders as a project maintainer by allowing you to automate tasks you'd otherwise have to take on yourself. The CI server can tell potential contributors not only whether their patches pass the project's tests but also how much those changes affect test coverage, compiled asset size, and any other metrics you care about.

Adding a CI server is a solid first step for project automation. You can go further by adding scripts to your contributors' development workflows and providing live documentation for developers to play with. Taking the time to set up all of these support tools will pay dividends by making your project's requirements crystal-clear to potential contributors and streamlining the process of reviewing their patches.

In this chapter, you'll learn to set up the popular Travis CI service to run the tests for the test-driven-carousel project. You'll also learn how to use Husky to add Git hooks to your project to check code before it's committed, spotting potential problems early. And finally, you'll generate sleek, interactive documentation for your carousel component with Storybook.

Setting up Travis CI

Travis CI is a continuous integration service that's become enormously popular in recent years, thanks to its convenience and versatility. Every time you or a collaborator pushes a change, Travis can run your project's scripts automatically and report the results through GitHub's Pull Request interface for branches. Each run is performed in its own isolated environment, producing more reliable results than you get in the personalized environment of a developer machine.

This section will walk you through the process of giving Travis CI access to your project, allowing you to offload tests and other automated tasks to the cloud. This will be a speedy process: you'll upload your project to GitHub, authorize Travis to access it, then add a configuration file to tell Travis to run your project's tests. Finally, you'll add a "badge" to show the world that your project's tests are passing on Travis CI.

Before proceeding, it's worth noting that Travis CI is a commercial product. When the first edition of this book was written, they offered a free plan that allowed you to use them with any public repositories. Unfortunately, that's no longer the case. As of this writing, the free plan is limited to active open source projects. For everything else, they offer a month-long free trial, which you'll need to cancel before it lapses if you want to avoid being charged. So if you want to follow along with this chapter, keep that in mind.

Hosting Your Project on GitHub

Travis CI is designed as an extension of GitHub, the preeminent source code hosting giant. If you don't already have an account with GitHub, now would be a good time to create one.[1] Once you're logged in, create a new repository for your personal incarnation of the test-driven-carousel project. Be sure to make it a public repository—Travis CI is free for public, open source projects. You can ignore all of the other options, as shown in the screenshot on page 125.

Once your repo is in place, GitHub will show you some command-line instructions for pushing an existing Git repository. Copy and paste those in the directory of the test-driven-carousel project from the last chapter:

```
$ git remote add origin git@github.com:TrevorBurnham/test-driven-carousel.git
$ git push -u origin main
Enumerating objects: 133, done.
```

---

1. https://github.com/

```
Counting objects: 100% (133/133), done.
Delta compression using up to 8 threads
Compressing objects: 100% (130/130), done.
Writing objects: 100% (133/133), 289.48 KiB | 6.58 MiB/s, done.
Total 133 (delta 64), reused 0 (delta 0)
remote: Resolving deltas: 100% (64/64), done.
To github.com:TrevorBurnham/test-driven-carousel.git
 * [new branch]      main -> main
Branch 'main' set up to track remote branch 'main' from 'origin'.
```

Create a new repository

A repository contains all project files, including the revision history. Already have a project repository elsewhere? Import a repository.

Required fields are marked with an asterisk (*).

Owner *   **Repository name ***

TrevorBurnham ˅   /   test-driven-carousel

◎ test-driven-carousel is available.

Great repository names are short and memorable. Need inspiration? How about urban-octo-parakeet ?

Description (optional)

Carousel component project from the book Test-Driven React

○   🔖 **Public**
Anyone on the internet can see this repository. You choose who can commit.

○   🔒 **Private**
You choose who can see and commit to this repository.

Initialize this repository with:

☐ Add a README file
This is where you can write a long description for your project. Learn more about READMEs.

Add .gitignore

.gitignore template: None ˅

Choose which files not to track from a list of templates. Learn more about ignoring files.

Choose a license

License: None ˅

A license tells others what they can and can't do with your code. Learn more about licenses.

ⓘ You are creating a public repository in your personal account.

Create repository

Congratulations—your project is now hosted by GitHub! By default, that means that anyone who's interested in your project can not only download a copy, they can also suggest changes by submitting a *pull request*. When they do, you'll want to know whether your tests pass against their suggested changes. That's where Travis CI comes in.

Adding a Travis Configuration

Next, use your GitHub account to log in to Travis CI.[2] Then give Travis the permissions it needs. Once you're logged in, you may be prompted to activate another layer of GitHub integration, GitHub Apps. Allow that too. If you're prompted to select a plan, choose the free trial plan.

Once Travis is able to connect to your GitHub account, you'll see a list of your GitHub repositories, including test-driven-carousel. Click the link to the repo's Travis page. At this point, there isn't much to see, because Travis doesn't know what you want it to do for the project.

To change that, you'll need a file at the root of test-driven-carousel called .travis.yml. The .yml extension indicates that this is a YAML[3] file, which is a minimal human-readable syntax for data. Tell Travis that you want to use Node v18 (the latest stable version as of this writing) and the "Jammy" Linux distribution, also known as Ubuntu 22 (the default Linux version is incompatible with recent Node versions):

```
dist: jammy
language: node_js
node_js:
  - 18
```

Commit and push this modest addition:

```
$ git commit -a -m ":wrench: Add Travis CI config"
$ git push
```

Now watch as the project's Travis page springs to life! (You may have to wait a minute or so.) Recognizing that test-driven-carousel is a Node project, it clones the project from GitHub, installs its dependencies from npm, then runs its tests for you:

```
$ npm test
> test-driven-carousel@0.0.0 test
> vitest
 RUN  v0.34.4 /home/travis/build/TrevorBurnham/test-driven-carousel
```

2.   https://travis-ci.com
3.   https://yaml.org

```
stdout | unknown test
 ✓ src/Carousel.test.tsx  (12 tests) 678ms
stdout | unknown test
 ✓ src/CarouselSlide.test.tsx  (6 tests) 59ms
stdout | unknown test
 ✓ src/CarouselButton.test.tsx  (3 tests) 29ms
 Test Files  3 passed (3)
      Tests  21 passed (21)
   Start at  23:19:21
   Duration  3.56s
```

Pretty cool, right? Although you should run your tests before pushing any changes, it's reassuring to see the tests pass when another machine downloads your commit. And if anyone submits a pull request against your project, Travis will automatically run your tests against that branch and report the result there.

Of course, a CI can do much more than run unit tests. To replace Travis CI's default npm test build script, add a script entry to your Travis config:

```
ch6/.travis.yml
dist: jammy
language: node_js
node_js:
  - 18
➤ script: npm test && npm run lint && npm run build
```

Now the CI will verify not only that your tests pass but that your code is lint-free and, most importantly, that it builds without errors. Commit this change:

```
:wrench: Define build script for Travis CI
```

Then push your code up to GitHub and watch the magic happen.

Adding a Status Badge

Let's add one final touch to our Travis integration. Right now, the result of Travis' latest test run is going to be tricky for anyone else to find. It's on a public but obscure Travis CI page. If your tests are passing, you should shout it from the rooftops! A common way to do that is to add a small image (known as a "badge") to the project README. Every time the badge loads, it shows the status of the latest build.

At the top of your project's Travis CI page, next to the project name, there should be a small image that says "build passing." That's the status badge. Click it to open a dialog where you can pick out an embeddable link. Choose Markdown from the format dropdown, then copy the little code snippet it generates.

Then create a README.md file in the root of your test-driven-carousel project. It's always a good idea for GitHub projects to have a README, since the README's contents are shown on the project's home page. Add a title, a short description, and the code you copied from Travis. The result should look something like this, with your GitHub username in place of username in the Build Status URLs:

```
ch6/README.md
# test-driven-carousel

[![Build Status](
  https://travis-ci.com/username/test-driven-carousel.svg?branch=main
)](https://travis-ci.com/username/test-driven-carousel)
```

Commit and push your changes using the Gitmoji for documentation:

```
$ git commit -a -m ":memo: Add README with status badge"
$ git push
```

Now your project's current build status will be displayed prominently on its GitHub page, as shown in the following screenshot.

That's it for our coverage of Travis CI. You can do lots more with Travis—tests are only the beginning! Travis can do just about anything you can write a script for. For more information, check out the Travis CI docs.[4]

Git Hooks with Husky

If you followed along with Chapter 2, Integrated Tooling with VS Code, on page 17, you've adopted a cutting-edge development setup, complete with integrated linting and autoformatting. However, your collaborators might not be so prepared. Nothing is stopping them from submitting a pull request that violates your project's prescribed ESLint or Stylelint rules or which will transform when you run it through Prettier. How can you enforce those rules?

---

4.   https://docs.travis-ci.com/

You could add checks to Travis CI, but then someone still has to fix the problems. Ideally, whoever introduced the problems should fix them *before* pushing their branch up for everyone else to see.

That's where Husky comes in. Husky is a tool for managing Git hooks in JavaScript projects. Git hooks are scripts that Git runs before or after certain commands, such as commit or push. In the olden days, developers had to install a project's Git hooks on their machine manually. Husky makes this much easier: when Husky is installed by npm (or yarn), it uses a post-install script[5] to install its own Git hooks, which will run whatever commands you specify for it in package.json. For developers working on your project, the process is effortless.

> ### Be Considerate with Hooks
>
> Git hooks are very powerful, and with great power comes great responsibility. Some project maintainers go overboard with hooks, forcing developers to run big, expensive scripts in the middle of their Git workflow. Respect your collaborators' time. If it takes more than a few seconds, consider making it a CI task rather than a Git hook.

Setting up Husky

Husky offers an npx script, husky-init, which performs its setup for you. By default, using npx to run a script that isn't already installed prompts you to (temporarily) install the package that contains the script. You can skip that confirmation step with the -y flag:

```
$ npx husky-init -y
husky-init updating package.json
  setting prepare script to command "husky install"
husky - Git hooks installed
husky - created .husky/pre-commit

please review changes in package.json
```

If you look at package.json, you'll notice a new entry in scripts:

```
// package.json
{
  ...
  "scripts": {
    "prepare": "husky install"
  }
  ...
}
```

---

5.   https://docs.npmjs.com/misc/scripts

The prepare script has a special meaning to npm—it runs automatically whenever someone runs npm install. Try it now:

```
$ npm install

> test-driven-carousel@0.0.0 prepare
> husky install

husky - Git hooks installed
```

Now when a new collaborator joins your project, they'll get the project's Git hooks automatically!

Take a look at the .husky/pre-commit script that Husky created. This is a shell script that, as its name implies, will run automatically before any Git commit. By default, it runs one command, npm test. That's not quite what we want. For one thing, Vitest's default test command starts in watch mode! For another, we want to run the linters, not just the unit tests. Automatically prettifying code would be nice too. So change the command to this:

```
#!/usr/bin/env sh
. "$(dirname -- "$0")/_/husky.sh"

➤ npm test -- --run && npm run format
```

The --run flag turns off Vitest's watch mode. The extra -- in front of it ensures that it's treated as an argument to Vitest, not to npm.

Now try committing:

```
$ git commit -a -m ":wrench: Add pre-commit hook"

> test-driven-carousel@0.0.0 test
> vitest --run

 ✓ src/CarouselButton.test.tsx (3)
 ✓ src/CarouselSlide.test.tsx (6)
 ✓ src/Carousel.test.tsx (12) 676ms

 Test Files  3 passed (3)
      Tests  21 passed (21)
   Start at  18:38:16
   Duration  1.25s

> test-driven-carousel@0.0.0 format
> npm run format:js && npm run format:css

> test-driven-carousel@0.0.0 format:js
> eslint --fix . && prettier --loglevel warn --write .

> test-driven-carousel@0.0.0 format:css
> stylelint "**/*.{ts,tsx}" --fix
```

```
[main 62727ae] :wrench: Add pre-commit hook
 3 files changed, 24 insertions(+), 2 deletions(-)
 create mode 100755 .husky/pre-commit
```

If there had been any test failures or errors, the commit would have been blocked, giving you the chance to fix the problems and try committing again. If you're familiar with shell idioms, Git is looking at the pre-commit hook's exit code (0 to indicate success, any other value for failure) to determine whether to allow the commit.

Skipping Git Hooks

If you're ever in a situation where you need to skip a Git hook—for example, if you need help resolving the linter errors you're seeing, so you want to commit to a branch you can share with your colleagues—run the Git command with the --no-verify flag.

And we're set! With this pre-commit hook in place, everyone who works on this project will have a much easier time finding out whether they're following its formatting standards.

We have one problem, though: even in this small package, the pre-commit hook feels a bit sluggish. Imagine how it would feel in a package with 10x or 100x as much code! Fortunately, there's a solution: instead of testing and linting the entire project, we can test and lint only the code that's changed.

Optimizing Pre-commit Hooks with lint-staged

The lint-staged[6] package is a popular tool for running scripts against staged files during pre-commit hooks. To get started with it, install lint-staged as a dev dependency:

```
$ npm install --save-dev lint-staged@14.0.1
```

Then add a new lint-staged section to package.json. This section takes the form of mappings from a glob pattern to a list of commands to run against staged files that match the pattern. We want to run our tests, plus all of the underlying commands from the format script. Here's the end result:

```
// package.json
{
  ...
  "lint-staged": {
    "*.{js,cjs,ts,tsx}": [
      "vitest related --run",
```

---

6.   https://github.com/okonet/lint-staged

```
      "eslint --fix",
      "stylelint --fix",
      "prettier --write"
    ]
  },
  ...
}
```

When lint-staged runs these commands, they have the same PATH as npm commands, so we can run package executables like vitest without having to preface them with npx. The vitest related command tells Vitest to only run against tests that have the staged files in their dependency tree, and the --run flag disables watch mode.

Finally, replace the command in the Husky pre-commit script with npx lint-staged:

ch6/.husky/pre-commit
```
#!/usr/bin/env sh
. "$(dirname -- "$0")/_/husky.sh"

npx lint-staged
```

Now to try it out! Commit these configuration changes:

```
$ git commit -a -m ":wrench: Use lint-staged to optimize pre-commit hook"
→ No staged files match any configured task
```

Since none of the files in the commit matched the glob pattern, we got to skip the pre-commit hook entirely. Now try adding a comment to, say, Carousel.tsx and making another commit:

```
$ git commit -a -m ":memo: Add comment to Carousel component"
✓ Preparing lint-staged...
✓ Running tasks for staged files...
✓ Applying modifications from tasks...
✓ Cleaning up temporary files...
```

Thanks to lint-staged, the pre-commit hook ran in a fraction of the time!

Congratulations—you've set up a top-notch pre-commit hook! Everything is in place to keep your codebase in ship-shape condition, without slowing down your workflow.

Adding Docs with Storybook

Now that you're sharing our project with the world, you should think about taking the documentation to the next level. Storybook[7] has rapidly become a popular library for generating documentation pages for React components.

---

7.   https://storybook.js.org/

Using Storybook, you can integrate live examples with all the information devs need to take full advantage of your components.

Getting Started with Storybook

Storybook has a handy script that you can run with npx to get started:

```
$ npx storybook@7.5.1 init
```

You'll see a few prompts. First, npx will confirm that you want to install storybook@7.5.1; type Y for Yes. Then you'll be asked if you want the Storybook ESLint plugin; type Y again.

Once the script finishes installing everything it needs, it should automatically start your project's Storybook server and open it in your browser:

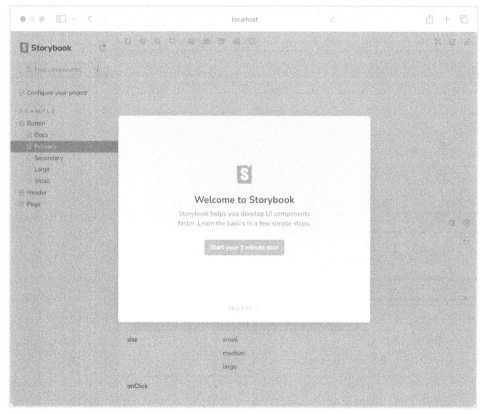

Go ahead and take the three-minute tour. Then come back to your editor and take a look at the changes in your project. In package.json, you'll see that you have several new devDependencies:

```
// package.json
...
"devDependencies": {
  ...
  "@storybook/addon-essentials": "^7.5.2",
  "@storybook/addon-interactions": "^7.5.2",
  "@storybook/addon-links": "^7.5.2",
  "@storybook/addon-onboarding": "^1.0.8",
  "@storybook/blocks": "^7.5.2",
  "@storybook/react": "^7.5.2",
  "@storybook/react-vite": "^7.5.2",
  "@storybook/testing-library": "^0.2.2",
  ...
},
...
```

You'll also see two new scripts:

```
// package.json
...
"scripts": {
  ...
  "storybook": "storybook dev -p 6006",
  "build-storybook": "storybook build"
},
...
```

That storybook script is what the init script ran to start the local Storybook server. Anytime you want to start it again, all you need to do is enter npm run storybook. The build-storybook script is used to compile your documentation into HTML, CSS, and JavaScript for deployment to the web (more on that later).

The script also added two new directories, .storybook/ and stories/. The .storybook directory contains configuration, and the stories/ directory is where your documentation will live. Right now stories/ has some placeholder documentation created by the init script, ready to be replaced with documentation for your own components. You can delete the contents of stories/ before proceeding.

Storybook docs are based on the concept of a "story," which is an example of a component. As the Storybook docs[8] put it:

> A story captures the rendered state of a UI component. Developers write multiple stories per component that describe all the "interesting" states a component can support.

Let's write a story for the Carousel component. Add a new module to stories/ called Carousel.stories.tsx:

---

8. https://storybook.js.org/docs/react/get-started/whats-a-story

```tsx
// stories/Carousel.stories.tsx
import type { Meta, StoryObj } from "@storybook/react";
import Carousel from "../Carousel";
import slides from "../example/slides";

const meta = {
  title: "Example/Carousel",
  component: Carousel,
} satisfies Meta<typeof Carousel>;

export default meta;
type Story = StoryObj<typeof meta>;

export const Basic: Story = {
  args: {
    slides,
  },
};
```

Moments after you save that, the change should immediately appear in the browser. Storybook's local server comes configured out of the box for hot module reloading (HMR), making updates very fast. The page receives the new JavaScript modules without having to refresh.

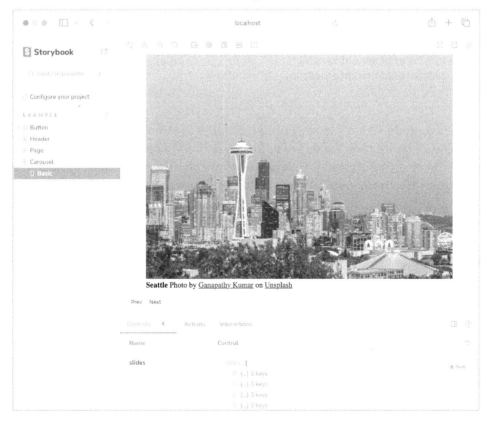

Seattle Photo by <u>Ganapathy Kumar</u> on <u>Unsplash</u>

This is a good time for a commit:

```
$ git commit -am ":wrench: Initial Storybook setup"
$ git push
```

Now you have a Storybook page that shows Carousel in action. But if that's all there was to it, there wouldn't be much reason to use Storybook instead of the project's existing preview script. So let's find out what else Storybook can do!

Enhancing Stories with Addons

The magic of Storybook is its extensibility in the form of assorted addons.[9] You'll find abundant options for making your documentation richer through these handy plugins.

Some of these addons have been included by default, as you may have gleaned from the project's devDependencies. You can see these declared in the Storybook config:

```
// .storybook/main.ts
...
addons: [
  "@storybook/addon-links",
  "@storybook/addon-essentials",
  "@storybook/addon-onboarding",
  "@storybook/addon-interactions",
],
...
```

The Essentials addon[10] is actually a collection of other popular addons, with built-in defaults that make sense for most Storybook projects. Let's take a closer look at two of them—Actions and Controls. These addons populate the first two tabs in the panel shown below each story.

The Actions addon[11] is simple: anytime an event handler prop is called, that call and its argument(s) are automatically logged in the Actions tab. Click the Next button three times and you'll see output like this (the most recent event is shown first):

```
onSlideIndexChange: 3
onSlideIndexChange: 2
onSlideIndexChange: 1
```

---

9. https://storybook.js.org/integrations
10. https://storybook.js.org/docs/react/essentials/introduction
11. https://storybook.js.org/docs/react/essentials/actions

That's all there is to it! You can manually set up individual callback props to trigger actions, but you generally don't need to, because the addon automatically binds all props that follow the onEvent naming convention.

The Controls addon[12] (formerly known as Knobs) is akin to a more stylish version of the props view in React Devtools. Open the Controls tab and you'll see the current value of each prop, and you can change those prop values in real time. For example, try changing the autoAdvanceInterval to 2000, and you'll see the slides advance every two seconds (with an accompanying onSlideIndexChange event noted in the Actions tab). If you get tired of the auto-advance, change it back to 0.

As with the Actions addon, the Controls addon offers quite a bit of customization, but it usually works fine out of the box, inferring the correct type of control to display from the prop type. But you'll come across one problem: notice that the slideIndex shown in the Controls tab doesn't change when you click Prev/Next; worse, if you change the slideIndex through the Controls tab, the Prev/Next buttons no longer work! (Incidentally, you may find that the values in the Controls tab stick around even after you hit refresh. Use the tiny reset icon in the upper-right corner of the tab to clear them.)

The problem is that Storybook has its own internal state, which is modifiable through the Controls tab and passed down to the component as *args* (Storybook's term for props). The component also has its own internal state, but that's overridden by props. So when slideIndex is set as a Storybook arg, it's no longer affected by the Prev/Next buttons. The solution is to write an onSlideIndexChange handler that modifies Storybook's slideIndex arg.

To modify args from a story, you'll need to change the way you render the story. Start by writing a render function that overrides Storybook's default render logic:

```
// stories/Carousel.stories.tsx
...
export const Basic: Story = {
  args: {
    slides,
  },
  render: function RenderCarousel(args) {
    return <Carousel {...args} />;
  },
};
```

---

12. https://storybook.js.org/docs/react/essentials/controls

That render function should produce the exact same story as before, but now we have the ability to intercept args and, crucially, to use hooks. Specifically, we'll need Storybook's useArgs hook:

```
// stories/Carousel.stories.tsx
import { useArgs } from "@storybook/preview-api";
...
export const Basic: Story = {
  args: {
    slides,
  },
  render: function RenderCarousel(args) {
    const [, updateArgs] = useArgs();

    return (
      <Carousel
        {...args}
        onSlideIndexChange={(newSlideIndex) => {
          // Update the slideIndex arg.
          updateArgs({ slideIndex: newSlideIndex });
          // Invoke the Actions addon handler.
          args.onSlideIndexChange?.(newSlideIndex);
        }}
      />
    );
  },
};
```

Now there's a two-way binding between the slideIndex Storybook arg and the slideIndex state in the component! Take a look at the example and you'll see that clicking Prev/Next modifies the slideIndex shown in the Controls tab, and you can freely switch back and forth between using those buttons and editing the slideIndex from the Controls tab.

We have just one more thing left to do with this story—publish it!

Deploying to GitHub Pages

So far, we've been using Storybook in dev server mode. It's time to put the project's story on the web where the world can see it! Shut down the dev server, then make one change to package.json: add the arg -o dist/storybook to the build-storybook script. That tells Storybook where to emit its build output. Now you have the final package.json for the chapter:

```
ch6/package.json
{
  "name": "test-driven-carousel",
  "private": true,
  "version": "0.0.0",
```

```
"type": "module",
"scripts": {
  "dev": "vite",
  "lint:js": "eslint . && prettier --list-different .",
  "lint:css": "stylelint \"**/*.{ts,tsx}\"",
  "lint": "npm run lint:js && npm run lint:css",
  "format:js": "eslint --fix . && prettier --log-level warn --write .",
  "format:css": "stylelint \"**/*.{ts,tsx}\" --fix",
  "format": "npm run format:js && npm run format:css",
  "build": "tsc && vite build",
  "test": "vitest",
  "preview": "vite preview",
  "prepare": "husky install",
  "storybook": "storybook dev -p 6006",
  "build-storybook": "storybook build -o dist/storybook"
},
"lint-staged": {
  "*.{js,cjs,ts,tsx}": [
    "vitest related --run",
    "eslint --fix",
    "stylelint --fix",
    "prettier --write"
  ]
},
"dependencies": {
  "react": "^18.2.0",
  "react-dom": "^18.2.0",
  "styled-components": "^6.0.5"
},
"devDependencies": {
  "@storybook/addon-essentials": "^7.5.2",
  "@storybook/addon-interactions": "^7.5.2",
  "@storybook/addon-links": "^7.5.2",
  "@storybook/addon-onboarding": "^1.0.8",
  "@storybook/blocks": "^7.5.2",
  "@storybook/react": "^7.5.2",
  "@storybook/react-vite": "^7.5.2",
  "@storybook/testing-library": "^0.2.2",
  "@testing-library/jest-dom": "^6.0.0",
  "@testing-library/react": "^14.0.0",
  "@testing-library/user-event": "^14.4.3",
  "@types/eslint": "^8.21.1",
  "@types/react": "^18.0.28",
  "@types/react-dom": "^18.0.11",
  "@typescript-eslint/eslint-plugin": "^5.58.0",
  "@typescript-eslint/parser": "^5.58.0",
  "@vitejs/plugin-react": "^4.0.4",
  "babel-plugin-styled-components": "^2.1.4",
  "eslint": "^8.35.0",
  "eslint-config-prettier": "^8.7.0",
```

```
    "eslint-plugin-react": "^7.32.2",
    "eslint-plugin-react-hooks": "^4.6.0",
    "eslint-plugin-storybook": "^0.6.15",
    "eslint-plugin-testing-library": "^6.0.1",
    "happy-dom": "^9.20.3",
    "husky": "^8.0.0",
    "jest-styled-components": "^7.1.1",
    "lint-staged": "^14.0.1",
    "postcss-styled-syntax": "^0.4.0",
    "prettier": "^2.8.4",
    "storybook": "^7.5.2",
    "stylelint": "^15.10.2",
    "stylelint-config-standard": "^34.0.0",
    "typescript": "^4.9.3",
    "vite": "^4.4.9",
    "vitest": "^0.34.4"
  }
}
```

You can run the script if you like, but you don't have to—we're going to make GitHub run it for us.

In the last few years, GitHub has added integrated CI functionality (similar to what Travis offers) in the form of GitHub Actions. As of this writing, that functionality is labeled as beta, but it's already the recommended way to deploy docs to GitHub Pages, and that type of action is provided as a free service.

To get started, you'll need to add a file that defines a *workflow* for GitHub Actions to run:

```
ch6/.github/workflows/static.yml
on:
  push:
    branches:
      - "main"

permissions:
  contents: read
  pages: write
  id-token: write

jobs:
  deploy:
    runs-on: ubuntu-latest
    steps:
      - id: build-publish
        uses: bitovi/github-actions-storybook-to-github-pages@v1.0.2
```

This configuration uses an action called Deploy Storybook to GitHub Pages,[13] which runs the build-storybook script for us and uses the output in dist/storybook/.

Commit those changes and push them:

```
$ git commit -a -m ":wrench Add workflow for GitHub Pages"
$ git push
```

Now you just need to enable GitHub Pages. Open the project's GitHub page and go to Settings. Navigate to the Pages screen. Under Source, select GitHub Actions. The workflow should kick off immediately.

It may take a minute or two for GitHub to run the workflow and publish your page. Once it finishes, you'll see a link at the top of the Pages settings screen. The address should be something like yourname.github.io/test-driven-carousel, and it should look just like what you saw locally when you ran the dev server. Now every time you push changes to the main branch, GitHub will update that Storybook page for you.

And with that, you've successfully automated the process of building and deploying documentation for your project!

Mantra: Actively Automate

In the field of web development, bugs stemming from hardware failure are truly rare. If something goes awry, then, in Hal 9000's famous words, "it must be human error." The task of building a bug-free website, then, is about minimizing human error. And with web-based applications growing ever more complex, we need all the help we can get. It's not enough to have good habits. If it can be done by software, software can do it more reliably than you can. So keep seeking out new ways to entrust development tasks to software. *Actively automate.*

In this final chapter, we've gone through some of the tools that have arisen in the last few years to help JavaScript developers with common tasks like running tests, linting, and generating documentation. Although this was a brief tour, I hope you came away from it with a strong sense of how you can automate away many of the chores you'd otherwise have to deal with as a software project maintainer.

---

13. https://github.com/marketplace/actions/deploy-storybook-to-github-pages

And that concludes our journey together. If you've developed a keener awareness of how your workflow impacts your work, then this book was a success. Because in the end, whether you're writing React components or any other kind of software, the path to becoming a better programmer is constant feedback. Treat every problem you run into as an opportunity to learn. Explore, experiment, play around. Never stop trying new things. Every expert started as a persistent novice.

Bibliography

[BM23]   Morten Barklund and Azat Mardan. *React Quickly, Second Edition*. Manning
         Publications Co., Greenwich, CT, Second, 2023.

[Gol22] Josh Goldberg. *Learning TypeScript: Enhance Your Web Development Skills
         Using Type-Safe JavaScript*. O'Reilly Media, Inc., Sebastopol, CA, First,
         2022.

Index

Thank you!

We hope you enjoyed this book and that you're already thinking about what you want to learn next. To help make that decision easier, we're offering you this gift.

Head on over to https://pragprog.com right now, and use the coupon code BUYANOTHER2024 to save 30% on your next ebook. Offer is void where prohibited or restricted. This offer does not apply to any edition of *The Pragmatic Programmer* ebook.

And if you'd like to share your own expertise with the world, why not propose a writing idea to us? After all, many of our best authors started off as our readers, just like you. With up to a 50% royalty, world-class editorial services, and a name you trust, there's nothing to lose. Visit https://pragprog.com/become-an-author/ today to learn more and to get started.

Thank you for your continued support. We hope to hear from you again soon!

The Pragmatic Bookshelf

Async JavaScript

With the advent of HTML5, front-end MVC, and
Node.js, JavaScript is ubiquitous—and still messy.
This book will give you a solid foundation for managing
async tasks without losing your sanity in a tangle of
callbacks. It's a fast-paced guide to the most essential
techniques for dealing with async behavior, including
PubSub, evented models, and Promises. With these
tricks up your sleeve, you'll be better prepared to
manage the complexity of large web apps and deliver
responsive code.

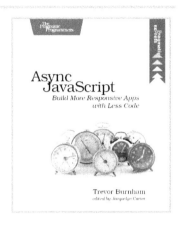

Trevor Burnham
(104 pages) ISBN: 9781937785277. $17
https://pragprog.com/book/tbajs

CoffeeScript

Over the last five years, CoffeeScript has taken the web
development world by storm. With the humble motto
"It's just JavaScript," CoffeeScript provides all the
power of the JavaScript language in a friendly and elegant package. This extensively revised and updated
new edition includes an all-new project to demonstrate
CoffeeScript in action, both in the browser and on a
Node.js server. There's no faster way to learn to write
a modern web application.

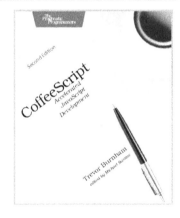

Trevor Burnham
(122 pages) ISBN: 9781941222263. $29
https://pragprog.com/book/tbcoffee2

Build Reactive Websites with RxJS

Upgrade your skill set, succeed at work, and above all, avoid the many headaches that come with modern front-end development. Simplify your codebase with hands-on examples pulled from real-life applications. Master the mysteries of asynchronous state management, detangle puzzling race conditions, and send spaceships soaring through the cosmos. When you finish this book, you'll be able to tame the wild code-beasts before they ever get a chance to wreck your day.

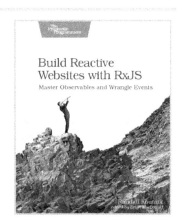

Randall Koutnik
(194 pages) ISBN: 9781680502954. $38.95
https://pragprog.com/book/rkrxjs

Web Development with ReasonML

ReasonML is a new, type-safe, functional language that compiles to efficient, readable JavaScript. ReasonML interoperates with existing JavaScript libraries and works especially well with React, one of the most popular front-end frameworks. Learn how to take advantage of the power of a functional language while keeping the flexibility of the whole JavaScript ecosystem. Move beyond theory and get things done faster and more reliably with ReasonML today.

J. David Eisenberg
(208 pages) ISBN: 9781680506334. $45.95
https://pragprog.com/book/reasonml

Rediscovering JavaScript

JavaScript is no longer to be feared or loathed—the world's most popular and ubiquitous language has evolved into a respectable language. Whether you're writing front-end applications or server-side code, the phenomenal features from ES6 and beyond—like the rest operator, generators, destructuring, object literals, arrow functions, modern classes, promises, async, and metaprogramming capabilities—will get you excited and eager to program with JavaScript. You've found the right book to get started quickly and dive deep into the essence of modern JavaScript. Learn practical tips to apply the elegant parts of the language and the gotchas to avoid.

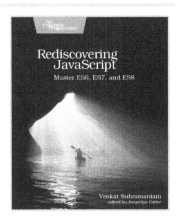

Venkat Subramaniam
(286 pages) ISBN: 9781680505467. $45.95
https://pragprog.com/book/ves6

Simplifying JavaScript

The best modern JavaScript is simple, readable, and predictable. Learn to write modern JavaScript not by memorizing a list of new syntax, but with practical examples of how syntax changes can make code more expressive. Starting from variable declarations that communicate intention clearly, see how modern principles can improve all parts of code. Incorporate ideas with curried functions, array methods, classes, and more to create code that does more with less while yielding fewer bugs.

Joe Morgan
(282 pages) ISBN: 9781680502886. $47.95
https://pragprog.com/book/es6tips

Programming Elm

Elm brings the safety and stability of functional pro-
graming to front-end development, making it one of
the most popular new languages. Elm's functional nature and static typing means that runtime errors are
nearly impossible, and it compiles to JavaScript for
easy web deployment. This book helps you take advantage of this new language in your web site development.
Learn how the Elm Architecture will help you create
fast applications. Discover how to integrate Elm with
JavaScript so you can update legacy applications. See
how Elm tooling makes deployment quicker and easier.

Jeremy Fairbank
(308 pages) ISBN: 9781680502855. $40.95
https://pragprog.com/book/jfelm

Learn Functional Programming with Elixir

Elixir's straightforward syntax and this guided tour
give you a clean, simple path to learn modern functional programming techniques. No previous functional
programming experience required! This book walks
you through the right concepts at the right pace, as
you explore immutable values and explicit data trans-
formation, functions, modules, recursive functions,
pattern matching, high-order functions, polymorphism,
and failure handling, all while avoiding side effects.
Don't board the Elixir train with an imperative mindset!
To get the most out of functional languages, you need
to think functionally. This book will get you there.

Ulisses Almeida
(198 pages) ISBN: 9781680502459. $42.95
https://pragprog.com/book/cdc-elixir

The Pragmatic Bookshelf

The Pragmatic Bookshelf features books written by professional developers for professional developers. The titles continue the well-known Pragmatic Programmer style and continue to garner awards and rave reviews. As development gets more and more difficult, the Pragmatic Programmers will be there with more titles and products to help you stay on top of your game.

Visit Us Online

This Book's Home Page
https://pragprog.com/book/tbreact2
Source code from this book, errata, and other resources. Come give us feedback, too!

Keep Up-to-Date
https://pragprog.com
Join our announcement mailing list (low volume) or follow us on Twitter @pragprog for new titles, sales, coupons, hot tips, and more.

New and Noteworthy
https://pragprog.com/news
Check out the latest Pragmatic developments, new titles, and other offerings.

Save on the ebook

Save on the ebook versions of this title. Owning the paper version of this book entitles you to purchase the electronic versions at a terrific discount.

PDFs are great for carrying around on your laptop—they are hyperlinked, have color, and are fully searchable. Most titles are also available for the iPhone and iPod touch, Amazon Kindle, and other popular e-book readers.

Send a copy of your receipt to support@pragprog.com and we'll provide you with a discount coupon.

Contact Us

Online Orders:	*https://pragprog.com/catalog*
Customer Service:	*support@pragprog.com*
International Rights:	*translations@pragprog.com*
Academic Use:	*academic@pragprog.com*
Write for Us:	*http://write-for-us.pragprog.com*